T0196327

POVERTY, PUBERTY, AND PRIDE

POVERTY, PUBERTY, AND PRIDE

A TEENAGE GUIDE

KITT FOXX

POVERTY, PUBERTY, AND PRIDE
A TEENAGE GUIDE

iUniverse books may be ordered through booksellers or by contacting:

iUniverse
1663 Liberty Drive
Bloomington, IN 47403
www.iuniverse.com
1-800-Authors (1-800-288-4677)

Because of the dynamic nature of the Internet, any web addresses or links contained in this book may have changed since publication and may no longer be valid. The views expressed in this work are solely those of the author and do not necessarily reflect the views of the publisher, and the publisher hereby disclaims any responsibility for them.

Any people depicted in stock imagery provided by Thinkstock are models, and such images are being used for illustrative purposes only. Certain stock imagery © Thinkstock.

ISBN: 978-1-4917-8736-6 (sc)
ISBN: 978-1-4917-8737-3 (e)

Library of Congress Control Number: 2016906262

Print information available on the last page.

iUniverse rev. date: 07/27/2016

PROLOGUE---- AND SHORT STORIES OF MY FIRST 17 YEARS.

This is a memoir of a child of the times -- born James Vernie Foster on November twenty third nineteen thirty four to a mother twenty one years of age, and a father twenty four years of age, in a two room share cropper shack on a ten acre farm in rural route two Woodstock Ga. Being born nineteen thirty four and growing up in this era when money was scarce and survival was a day to day challenge to many, a lot of different ways to cope with the poverty of the times were invented, and tried by my young generation, some legal, some not so legal, but we were poor, but determined. Puberty was a very confusing thing, and often caused us to do inappropriate things in pursuit of our goals, credibility of our acts were questioned by our old fashioned parents, but our fierce, determined pride, demanded us to break some old rules and we started a new and different era in the forties and fifties and this is the story of how much desperation we were in at that time and how we were able to survive, our pent up aggressiveness and still be able to retain our place in society later in our lives. Poverty, Puberty, and Pride continued to torment my life up until about the age of seventeen until my evolvement into manhood, a long hard and difficult struggle was behind me.

TRYING TO SURVIVE 1934-1941.

My mom Mary Lou Grimes Foster and I were mudded in for the winter a lot of the time, there were little or no road maintenance crews in nineteen thirty four thru nineteen forty one in the winter,. My dad James Allen Foster worked in Atlanta from Thirty nine until forty one and in the winter he drove the car as close as he could to home usually the roads became so terrible that he had to park it and walk the next few miles to us at the farm, most of the roads were impossible to use in the winter time, the roads were dirt, and full of deep holes of. Mud and water getting stuck was not good.

It rained in the winter in Ga. and at times we got sleet, snow, ice storms, and we had a generous supply of red mud. My dad did not own a car so he had to borrowed one from his uncle Raymond for long periods of time. Our farm was about thirty eight miles north of Atlanta and the house was not insulated at all, it was very cold except in front of the fireplace, when the wind blew, cold air came up thru the cracks in the wooden floor, winters were not the best of times in the rural areas of Georgia, in the thirties. I do know that the farm cost nine hundred dollars. Forty five acres a house and barn with ten acres in pasture, lots of trees and a nice spring fed Creek in the pasture and an orchard of apples and peaches about fifteen of each and a mixture of varieties of each it was a great little farm and, boy did we need helicopters back in those days, for impossible to reach some areas, necessity truly was the mother of invention. Mom and I were raising broiler chickens in the early forties, and full time farmers in most of the forties also. We fed and watered the chickens three times a day, and raised cotton and corn crop in our spare time in the summer, and hoed the weeds from the crops after the summer rains.

Dad would plow the fields and plant the corn, cotton, and the vegetable garden in the spring, on the weekends if he could get home weather permitting our old mule earned his keep in the hot humid weather, only the spring rains let him stay in the barn, my mom knew how to hitch up a mule to a plow just as good as my dad, and how to use it.

He then went back to Atlanta to work after spring planting, back to the garage in the Atlanta area repairing and maintaining a fleet of trucks for a large ice and coal company, mom and i stayed on the farm and tended the crops. We also had to draw water from a deep well at the edge of our yard via a rope and windlass hand cranked by mom and we carried it about one hundred yards in buckets to the thirsty chickens, many times we wanted to sit down and rest but we couldn't, there was just too much that had to be accomplished. Caring for the birds, those were not the good ole days that people refer to. We worked very hard from daylight till dark, if we made three bales of cotton and sixty bushels of corn that was a darn good season for us, plus we raised out two or three houses full of eight thousand chickens each. In the same season cleaned out the manure and spread it out over the farmland to be plowed under later next spring by dad. That was our fertilizer for the next year's crop and if a crop was successful it needed this fertilizer each year. Early to bed and early to rise, the way our Spring and Summers were always on on the farm. Eight hundred to twelve hundred dollars was our annual income from the farm. Dads salary was almost two thousand dollars per year so our total was about three thousand dollars per year in Thirty nine thru. Forty One. Less the taxes.

HOME LIFE 1939.

Farming was not a paying occupation for us, it was extremely hard work and barely supplying us with the necessaries of life. Chicken farming was an additional income method for our survival in those trying times so I can can say that in my childhood years, when I was four to seven years old, I knew about hard work. My mom was a very hard worker and I tried to be as much help to her as a small boy could be, so I became a cotton picking, chicken feeding little guy early on in my life. Her young life was no different, her father was a farmer also and working the fields was required as a part of life.It was all we knew.

Peaches, apples, strawberries and wild muscadines were available in plentiful amounts on the property in season, we gathered and ate what we wanted and were able to secure for ourselves. Other foods in season (muscadines are wild thick skinned grapes and grew up in the trees on a long vine) you had to shake the vine really hard and they rain down on you, then you pick em up and eat em up, back then the woods were full of them in the summer and they were such a treat. There were other wild fruits such as persimmon, sugar berries, and wild plums to be had for the taking. Blackberry's and dewberry's we're excellent pie fillings, summers were good times back then. Even in our hard times we managed to be happy-go-lucky and enjoy life. The problems of the world were far far away from us in the late thirties and early forties our days were concerned with survival and the coming winter and the preparation for for the lean times ahead.

STAYING WARM 1939.

In the Late thirties, when I was six--seven years old, in the winter time mom and i would hang the quilting frames from hooks up on the living room ceiling, and start preparing to make some more quilts, these were a good bartering item at the stores when other items were plentiful and the seasons were changing and warm sleeping materials were now the next concerned items, so many things to be done as the weather became decidedly cooler at night. Mom would get out her sewing machine and locate all the old scraps of material that were saved for this purpose and start sewing the quilt tops together. Then we put the batting in (a thin layer of cotton) in the center, roll up the bottom on the frames and start to hand sew the three pieces together making a quilt. Some winters we would make three or four quilts. Mom had names for the designs that we created on each one, they were beautiful when we finished them, but many many hours were involved to make these quilts and each one with a different design. Mom was very good with the designs, many years of helping her mom had given her the experience, and at the age of six I had helped my mother each winter with the quilt making process, so much as she permitted.

I had my own needle and thimble for hand sewing and each and every stitch had to pass moms inspection or take it all out and start all over again. So I got pretty good at it after lots and lots of practice. If we had chickens at the time we had to stop to feed and water them as needed, they were used to being fed and watered at a regular times each day and made lots of noise if we were late,. Then go back to our quilting, there was always quilting frames hanging in our cozy living room in front of the fireplace. In winter some of those quilts were unequivocally gorgeous to feel and just to look at. Mom was quite an expert seamstress back in those days and some of those were a true work of art, they were truely beautiful..I was a proud little guy to say that I helped.

WORKING THE FIELD 1944

In the fall we pulled the corn fodder (the leaves of the corn plant) from the dried out corn stalks and tied them into shocks, (about one hundred) or more leaves of fodder per shock with two leaves folded together and wrapped around and tucked in tight to keep it together. These were then hauled in the mule drawn wagon to the barn and placed into the loft for use of food for the milk cow, it was good feed for the cow, we also saved peanut and potato vines for the cow, they made the milk a little sweeter and the cow loved them. Milking the cow was another thing that I had to master with mom's help, the cow didn't seem to like me and and at times it was not possible, it was a learning process for us both. She finally accepted me and all was well, one thing less for mom to do and another milestone for me at 6 years old. Milk was an important food source and was used in many ways, butter made from the milk was a good barter item at stores for things we needed in the kitchen. Then in the fall all corn stalks must be cut down, piled up and burned. The cotton stalks got the same treatment. Now if we had any surplus chicken manure stashed along the edge of the fields, this is when it was spread manually, by shoveling it into and out of the wagon, on to the fields by mom and I, hauled there via the mule and wagon, to be plowed under by dad next spring.

PREPARATION AND HOME CANNING 1939

Now the cotton picking and fertilizing was done, all the chicken manure removed from the chicken house and spread or stashed out somewhere along the fields, the harvest of the spuds (potatoes) both kinds (sweet and Irish) begin. They must be pulled and or dug up from the soil and the potato hill created. First we dug out a hole in the earth about twelve fourteen inches deep and create a teepee type of structure with boards, then covered it with an old piece of tar paper or an old piece of linoleum floor covering (we never threw anything useable away) filled the interior with wheat or pine straw mixed in with the potatoes, then covered the potatoes until needed (apples could be kept in with the potatoes) or until used that winter because if they froze they rotted and were not eatable, so with about four to five inches of a dirt layer on top of the hill, this kept ole Jack Frost and the cold from our spuds and apples, we also fashioned a small little trap door so we could get to them as needed later in the winter. This method was used in many cases because there was no other storage method available at the time to keep them from freezing. Alot went into the root cellar for safe keeping by those who had root cellars, however we were not that fortunate. We did have a storm cellar that we used for a root cellar in the winter for some things.such as kraut, and some canned goods.

We had a garden every year with lots of veggies and melons, we picked a lot of wild berries and we had fields full of corn to eat. It was lots of work to be self sufficient on the farm and there were some things like salt, sugar, coffee, and other items necessary for your kitchen that had to be bartered for with butter and eggs and sometimes smoked hams and bacon were traded also.

Mom also dried lots of peaches and apples in the fall for fruit pies later in the winter. We had about fifteen peach trees & the same amount of apple trees, lots of fruit. Once the berries, fruits and veggies ripened the canning season began, and each of us had our share of things to do. My little brothers job was to stay out out of the way haha. Home canning is lots of work. Usually most things that were canned or pickled have to be packed into clean sterile jars, packed into the big wash pots outside, each jar isolated from each other by towels, rags, or socks, and boiled for for a period of time, then removed, wiped clean, and the lids re tightened, and placed upside down on a quilt and covered with another to cool down slowly. After about four to five days each one is inspected for very small bubbles. If any are detected that jar will spoil so it must be opened and eaten. As you know you got to string and snap the green beans, shell the peas before canning, and dry the pinto and butter beans before storing them. Peaches were pickled along with beets and cucumbers and they go thru the same process to be pickled and home canned. Usually fall is a very demanding time, canning is time consuming, With all the other chores that must be done daily with the livestock, chickens, and pigs. At At night your back reminded you that you had a hard day.

HOG KILLING TIME 1940

Sometime in January when its going to be zero degrees for a week or so, my dad and uncle Jim killed the hogs, we usually had two. Now for the next few weeks mom canned, cooked sausage, liver, and tenderloins for later use. It was awfully cold outside for me so I got to turn the crank on the sausage grinder as mom mixed the salt and herbs in and fried it out. These things could be "cold packed", meaning they did not have to be boiled in the jars. Lots of grease that was cooked out of the meat, or melted lard, was used for the purpose of sealing the contents by poring it over the meat before the lids were screwed on tightly and placed in an area that would not freeze. An area underground that doubled as shelter during the tornado season next summer.worked fine. It was a large area that things stored there didn't freeze.

Dads job was to prepare the hams and shoulders that were put in the smokehouse with the bacon and chop cuts, on hangers of wire or strings, and start the good smelling hickory smoking process. The rest was put into a large wooden box filled with salt and a hinged cover built for keeping and preserving the meat by curing it in salt. If this sounds like a lot of trouble and work it is, but your food supply must be prepared with care. Wood cutting was a dangerous man's job. Dad and my uncle Jim preformed this duty early every fall for both households, cutting and sawing hardwood trees and splitting it into firewood for the fireplace and into shorter lengths for the kitchen stove. This had to be done early in the fall to let the wood wood dry out so it would burn hotter. Wet wood don't burn it smokes, wet hickory wood, that's what was used in the smoke house to cure the hams and bacon with hickory smoke. This was a yearly event.

STAYING HEALTHY 1939

From nineteen thirty four to nineteen fifty four life was a struggle for people in good health, and sadly a lot of good people, not on on a proper diet, died for no reason other than working themselves beyond their endurance, but survival depended on it, and failing to prepare for winter was also not a condition that you could expect to turn out good, so they continued doing so until they dropped, got very sick and died, only the strong survived, and if you are alive today you may owe your ancestor's a debt of gratitude for your existence. Back in the thirtys if you did not prepare for winter you could starve or freeze.or move in with relatives for the season. A full winters supply of firewood and food are necessary, wood had to be cut and dried before winter or you were in big trouble, country living was hard and staying warm helped in staying healthy.

HARD TIMES 1939

People in the city were different, I don't know how they survived. But, Because they had jobs, grocery stores, money, natural gas for heat and much nicer and warmer homes than up in the sticks. But out in the sticks we were prepared, that was a fact of life if you were to survive the winter. "Being a cotton picking chicken farmer" was hard work, some of my life and a lot of my moms was very difficult back in those days, the great depression was known as Hard Times and they were. A dime was a lot of money in nineteen thirty four thru nineteen forty one, five to seven dollars per day was good wages then, if you could find a job. This was a time in which neighbors helped each other with farm life without expecting anything except a return in kindness, nobody had money until the cotton was picked and sold to pay off your debts for the last year..Being a good neighbor, and having good neighbors was the Christian thing to do back then, and it it was practiced.

THE WAR 1941

Things changed drastically in forty two when we were at war, wages went up and so did prices, many things were not available even if you had the money, the new hard times were on us now. We had another struggle coming, if we had only known. WW2 was a fact, suddenly one cold, snowy December the seventh, nineteen forty one, Sunday morning in Georgia. The bombs fell on Pearl Harbor Hawaii. Up until that happened the most exciting thing that had happened was the cow got out of the pastures somewhere, and mom and I were out half the night looking for it by lantern light that was a "happening" to us. And milking a stupid cow at two A.M. in the morning was not one one of our favorite things, especially if she had been eating bitter weed or. wild onions, and ruined the milk.

WAR.

WW 2

December seventh Forty One It was war!!! and everyone was so afraid that our love ones were at risk. And I had no idea what lay in store for me in my future no idea what poverty was, or that we were already in it, and having to move to another home south toward Atlanta had no meaning to me at the time. Only later when I started to school did the word poverty mean any thing, or affect me personally, and emotionally, but some kids were cruel, and that's when it dawned on me that compared to other kids we were not as educated in things that city kids were, this was all completely different to me and mom had to to send us to school with the clothes we had, and we were in trouble.

my world begin to change. Being laughed at as a a hick was was not funny, The uncertainty of what's next was always on our parents minds, and even at the age of seven I knew they were very worried.about the war.and the changes it would bring into into our lives.and there were many.moms that was afraid dads would be drafted and she could not drive a car, that was the.reason for moving to Sandy Springs in early forty two, for us, dad had to go to Fort Mack for a week and take his physical for for the military, but because dad. Had fallen into the hog pen. When he was a.boy about fifteen and broke his arm, his mom just wrapped it up and it healed crooked, that kept him from being drafted into the army, he was deferred as four F. So he got a job building. B29 bombers at. Bell Aircraft in. Marietta. Ga.for the duration of the war.

SUNDAY SCHOOL 1939

Out here on the farm there were endless things that must be done seven days a week fifty fifty-two weeks a year, most of the time except very cold winter days we walked to church on Sunday morning after chores were done starting about five am it was only two miles thru the woods to the Methodist Church and seven miles to the Baptist church (Summer time church) so mom chose the close one.mom wrapped up my baby brother in his blankets, and out thru the woods we went on sunny Sunday mornings. I could never tell the difference from from the Baptist church, Sunday schools were the same in my oplnion.even some of the other kids expressed the same view, it wasn't important to us kids, sometimes if my grandfather Foster was preaching the sermon mom and I would stay for the services, A lot of those old people were praying for a better nicer, safer, world and we are living in what they prayed for today., before going back home, and on occasion just maybe get a ride home home in grandfather's thirty seven Ford, now that was a treat.and just maybe he would stop at the store and buy me an Orange Crush.drink. that was a real treat for me, and mom also.My grandfather Foster was a very quiet religious man, that never said anything bad about anyone. and read his bible constantly. And delivered a sermon as the minister two Sundays each month. A good and honorable man.

HOUSE WORK AND LITTLE BROTHER 1938

There was the cow to be fed and milked two times a day the mule the pigs had to be fed,, the eggs to gather, the garden to be hoed, the washing to be done. Summer and winter, and clothes to be hung out on the clothesline to dry,, food to be cooked, floors to be swept, and floors to be mopped,, milk to be churned, butter to be made and molded, Whether it was cold or hot, good thing i was equipped to pee standing up --cause if i had ever sat down it would have been over for me, and then there was my baby brother three years younger born in nineteen thirty seven. Someone's gotta watch and entertain him in the spring and summer, the fields won't wait, the grass is growing and must be removed. mom would park him in the shade somewhere, and my job was to shoo the flies and keep the ants off him. while she worked the field i was only four or five at that time but i remember when he got older he was tied from the waist to a tree and put on a quilt while mom and i worked the fields. He could "shoo" his own flies and ants.by then.

A bucket of water sitting over in the shade and a dipper was our salvation on a hot summer day drink some, pour some over your head. In them cornfields and cotton fields down in rural Georgia in nineteen thirty nine an old straw hat helped, but it was hot and humid work, that much I remember well.

Lunch was a chunk of cold cornbread and some cold pinto beans and at times a baked sweet potato and a glass of cool milk drawn up from the wells cool water. Anything is good after six hours of hoeing weeds and grass in the corn rows, on on a hot muggy day in Georgia.

ELECTRIC POWER 1941

We had no electric power until nineteen forty one when the R E A brought us electric power. We had no idea what a refrigerator was couldn't afford one anyways, so milk and butter were placed in the well bucket and lowered into the well just carefully touching the water, the same for anything you wanted to keep cool a sixty five ft. Deep well that served as our refrigerator as it had for my mom and dad when they grew up it was all that was known at that time, other people used root cellars or natural springs or a source of cool flowing water for natural cooling since time began. Some people owned ice boxes but what good was an ice box back then to us, when when the closest ice was twenty miles away. Ice in the summer was a rare treat to us.

We got ice in.the winter that had to do for the year. Ice in the summer meant someone else had to bring it to us, Mom and I had no way to go get, and no money to buy ice, or any place to store it for later use, if we had any. Things were different back then, we had to do without many things that are very common today, and we had to make it, grow it, or barter for it if we had it, no money and no ice. Some of those hot humid muggy days we if we had money would have gladly paid for a glass of ice cold sweet tea. Maybe all this excitement when I was so young prepared me for what was to come in the future we were living in Dulls ville,. and didn't realize it and living in poverty already, we were.what was known back then as "getting by" in those days, and thought that was good.

BAD WATER 1939

On occasion an ole black snake would fall into the well, and regardless of what they do about these things in Texas and Oklahoma (they cook them)we tasted and smelled the difference in our water a few days after his swim went bad, whew! nasty this was a disaster, if we had no chickens because they needed lots of water, the well water level would be drawn down rapidly, and this lower level of the water in the well would increase the chances that the snake would be brought up intact earlier before we noticed the difference in taste, Chickens drink lots of water, and we had No chickens at that time so, luck was not in our favor, that means that plan two had to be placed into effect, and that plan was not the desirable one to either mom or myself It was dangerous, and the very thought of going into a deep dark well alone was awful, however, the well had to be drawn dry, or close to dry as possible and then someone must get in the bucket and be lowered down into the well and find the culprit and send him topside or do without water, so a choice had to be made mom and I the only people for miles, so me being much lighter than my mom. Didn't leave us much choice, that first time that had me going into the well at six years old was terrifying, but it must be done, if you can't trust your mother who can you trust? (same thoughts i had when she wanted me to crawl under the barn and confront a mean old setting hen) under the barn floor.

Mom looked worried and I was scared, but. flash light in my hand and the other one hanging on for dear life, and tears in my eyes, down and down I went and mom calling to me that it was OK, To hold on tight and don't sway the bucket and fall out of it, finally-after what seemed forever i was there and saw the snake, mom said pick it up put it in the bucket. Then she drew it up to her, then lowered the bucket back down to me, and instructed me to get back into the bucket, and slowly,. drew me back up, And into her arms and some fresh air and after we both stopped crying she hugged me tightly kissed me and said that I was her "little man," It would take hours for the well to recover its water level again. After that first time I went into the well it was a-piece a cake.

NEW FEELINGS 1949

You got a lot of nerve young man!-----I never knew what the heck they were in reference to but that experience has come in handy many times in my life and later, it helped me in many ways in not being afraid to try something I wanted to do but was hesitant to try, but things got easier as I grew older and bolder, _we made a little money raising the chickens, later. Because we had fifty thousand or more, after moving to another house that i. named the chicken ranch, three huge chicken houses with with the ability to have eighty thousand at one time, this was mom's idea, full time chicken farm.

I got enough nerve to drive my cousins crude little race car so I became a pretty good race car driver at fifteen I always wanted to so why not, Saturday nite I was a dirt track racing fool a few Saturday nights In the summer my mom didn't approve of this and, my dad didn't know it, it was a close call at times to keep the car hidden at one of_my friend's home, they had a Sioux war bonnet painted on top of the old race car because They said that I drove like a wild Indian going to s. --t but I really enjoyed the thrill and excitement of it, it was addictive to me, and i knew that some day I had to race with the big boys, but i never had a car or a sponsor with that kind of money.but I dreamed!!!!

Maybe those trips into that well when i was a youngster did have some effects, that I was not aware of at that age, I did kinda became a little daredevil and being the adventures type spelled trouble for me in life but I won a few trophies racing, its a good way to improve your driving skills if you have the nerve to do it and i loved it, and and had my own later in life and later had to make a couple of other trips into some other deep wells also later to remove a hen, and a dead cat out before they completely ruined the. water for people, it became known that at age 12 I could and would go in and clean them out for you.always for a. Fee or not, the thrill of doing something that grown men were afraid to do, was payment enough, it got to be actually fun for me.

HAVEING FUN 1940

I think my adventurous nature helped me conquer, or at least helped me deal with being afraid of some things, I'm sure that not anyone of my friends or acquaintances had ever tried or experienced a trip into a water well at that age. Mom was very good at convincing me to do things I didn't really want to do, I'm sure she did not want me to get paranoid about them, and I didn't., in fact I think it had the opposite effect, older and bolder,

The trips into the wells i made were an educational experience and had that not been so necessary, would never ever happened. But i did not realize that at the tender age of six, I don't remember being afraid of a lot of things that other boys were, like snakes, (i got bit three times) graveyards, teachers, bullies, carnival rides, swimming pool diving boards, heights,-girls, mostly kid stuff like playing the game of pine top fox at the age of twelve,. -twenty or twenty five--feet up in the tree tops one guy the fox(usually me) everyone else the dogs, -you gotta catch me ha--ha-- no one ever did I was like a squirrel up there, I was always a gutsy little dude, or a crazy one which ever you prefer.

SEX 101----1940

Then there were girls--I found out we were remarkable different when i was six, no no no it was not my idea it was hers, I won't mention her name, she was also six but she had been doing strange things to me at school and i think, molesting me, maybe she had been watching (porno mom and dad) at home some nights and had decided to re-enact those same things with me in the barn loft, so i learned the basics before she finished with me that afternoon and I was not too excited about it at the time-in nineteen forty ----but have, mended my ways about things of that nature and as of the present day, there are three boys two girls that now call me dad, now, and I love and cherish them all, five kids Will keep you busy, Right Dave, Neva, Dan, Veronica, and Joe??

CHIGGERING LITTLE ODIE 1939

When the Black Berries were ripe in the summer, mom would ask me and my brother Troy. to go find some for a big cobbler pie, now that's a pie crust on the bottom of the deep pan, filled halfway another crust in the middle, more filling and a crust on top, takes lots of blackberries to make one that the way we liked it but out there with the Berry's is a little red monster called a "Chigger," he is so tiny you can't see him but they are blood suckers and burrow down into your skin, And the next day when it gets hot and you get a little sweaty, guess who starts to itch like crazy? Yep, the little red bug, and you can't see him but you sure know he is there, and a swim in the pond won't dislodge him, you can't stop scratching, finally a bump appears on your skin now you can locate his butt, some kerosene dabbed on him in the bump usually kills him but the bump itches for another few days or so, just hope some of them don't get into your underwear, or in that area, that is a hard place so scratch without other people noticing and some smart ass around will make fun of you then always ask if you have crotch crickets.You just have to avoid people for the duration of the "chigger". It was really a chore to get those Berry's every year, but those pies were a real treat to eat. And a few chiggers were not going to stop us from the blackberry season, mom was lucky she had 2 boys that loved those pies!.but if they got under your arms and you sweated any at all it was awful, those little noseeums would drive you nuts, and it was terrible for a few days after the pie was gone, boy it is embarrassing even at the age of seven or eight for your mom to make you lie down naked out on the front porch in the sunlight so she can inspect your private areas for chiggers and dab a little kerosene on the "Chiggering" little "Oddie" area she called it, and made fun of us.my mom was one of a kind. But it sure saved us lots of scratching and itching later that week or longer, and if you scratched too hard and got infected it was even more trouble to heal in that area, if you got hot and sweaty it would drive you crazy itching. So she always cautioned us when heading out to pick blackberries to put some kerosene on our shirt sleeves and pants seams to help ward off the little chiggers, it didn't stop them all but it sure did help. Mom knew these things. and it saved us the embarrassing ordeal of having mom "Chigger little Oddie"! Again.

MANNERS MATTER 1949

Its hard to be a country boy and live in town, you only have overalls to wear and clod hoppers for shoes, dad could only afford one pair of shoes a year and we wore thru our overalls on our knees mom would put patches on them, luckily we were not the only ones dressed like that, but most of the other kids were dressed much nicer and I was ashamed that I had to be like that, some boys made fun of us and usually wound up with a bloody nose in payment for the lack of manners. After I got older and opened up the bank of prince Albert (I will explain this later)) I bought me some bell bottoms with the laces in the back some nice shirts and a v neck sweater penny loafers shoes, told my mom it was my grass cutting money. And that suited her and dad fine one less thing to worry about. And most of the girls didn't mind if I hung out with them then. Also just feeling better about myself seemed to improve my attitude. I truly don't think that my mom and dad realized the peer pressure we faced at school dressed like we were.it was only because of our financial situation at home.Im sure mom would would have loved to have seen. Us dress nicer in school as the other other kids did.if the money had been available we we would have I'm sure.

THE SHOWER 1946

I finally stopped sleeping with my brother in the summer I slept down on the floor after he went to sleep and on hot nights I went out the window and slept on the front porch. With no way to bathe, I finally rigged up a shower with the garden hose out between the chicken house and the feed house with some old canvas that I found at the dump as front and back of the area. and the whole family used it in the summer, I also found an old wooden pallet to stand on so we were not making a mud hole out there and mom made my brother shower every morning., because he wet the bed, and usually wet me also and I hated that,. I was so glad when Dad finally got.mom a wringer type washing machine on credit at the Firestone store down in Buckhead, (north Atlanta) it was out on the back porch in the summer and the kitchen in the winter so she could wash the sheets, under ware, and blankets, on bros bed every day. And. dry them in the kitchen.poor mom.I don't know how she did it.and sometimes I still wondering how she and I managed to run a farm back in the late thirtys.mom left us in two thousand and one she she won't have to struggle with life's problems any longer.

She was eighty eight when she went away. A long hard life. But a lot of accomplishments in her time on this earth.seven of us, five boys two girls all grown up. "fat and sassy" as she would say! Miss You Mom, she was always my best friend we did so much together on the farm and with the chickens. She was a worker, made us boys look bad, when there was work to be done. She never ask us boys to do anything she would not do herself.she was very instrumental in instilling a sense of pride and accomplishment in all of us, that has served us all well.and good work ethics have been been the key to all of her children's success.

WATER. GOOD. AND BAD 1940

The water that we drank and cooked with always came from a well out in the toolies in Georgia, it was necessary that it had to be protected from the elements, also snakes, chickens, cats, and kids they ruined the taste of the water (kids especially)and also rain water running into a well created contamination and was not safe to drink or cook with, any topsoil being washed into it from the yard where the chickens, dogs, and kids, walked around made it unsafe to give to our other animals or even the hot house chickens, so a shelter was put over it called a "curb" similar to a large box with a square hole on top with cover that sealed the big well hole from the critters, or small children,.or one of moms hens, from falling into it. A small ditch was dug to help the flow of water go away from the curb.. And dirt was placed along the curb area to keep water from going underneath the curb into the well. A good well was always the success or failure of a farm. Sick people don't work good. And bad Water can also eventually kill you.The depth of a well depended on the underground water table And that varied from location to location some were only twenty five feet deep others were eighty feet or more, ours was sixty sixty-five feet deep. The deeper the cooler the water seemed to be. Some produced tremendous volumes of water, some filled slowly, we were fortunate that ours had excellent flow and was deep.and our water had good taste if your well was considered a good one it increased the value of your property or farm a good well was a necessity for health and well being in those days if it had a rock bottom that was blue granite you were drinking water that might contain arsenic and over a period of years you usually went slowly blind because of that my dad's father had that happen to him my grandfather Foster was blind before sixty and his arsenic level was very high his doctor told my dad it was from his well water. The water was tested and it was confirmed. Dad lowered a string of dynamite into it and collapsed it sealed it with cement and warned in the wet cement that this well was contaminated with arsenic and not to reopen it.

No water made it necessary to abandon the home and build another miles away, But before the testing was available for this as a public service how many hapless people in the past. centuries prematurely were blinded or died from this? No one knows!! Really Sad. But everyone needed water.but no one in those days would have considered the well water to be a cause of that. People just didn't think that was possible, It also seemed that shallow wells were prone to be muddy or the water tasted muddy, and if the taste was not acceptable a new well was dug in a different location and in some instances powdered lime was used to improve the clarity and taste of it, if it was really bad, the water was hauled from a neighbor's clear water well for household use. And a farm or dwelling with a "sour well" was hard to sell.and only a greenhorn would buy something like that. Most people bragged about things like a good well on the homestead.The hazards that people in that time period faced were not recognized sometimes until it was too late, like my grandfather Foster..

MAKEING. MONEY THE THE HARD WAY

To a country boy Saturdays were the special days, work is over and it's fun time, if dad would allow me to use his truck to go. On a date with my girl friend, on Saturday night, which was only only an excuse to make a moonshine run to Atlanta and at a dollar per case seventy five dollars was was easy money for that lots, and lots of times after picking her up we just rode around in town before loading up up and heading for Atlanta, on a good night two trips were possible, one hundred fifty dollars was was my pay, that money went into my prince Albert can. Up in the cemetery, along with the funds from my sales of the.stove wood and produce we had sold in Atlanta previously that same day. Stove wood and produce selling in Atlanta on Saturday am was. another enterprise that we three boys did did to make money, and I had to hide it from my parents to stay alive, Because my dad would have beat me to death if if he if he had known what I was doing, Because he was only making about forty five dollars per week, working five and a half days per week, and I'm only sixteen and making about two hundred and fifty dollars dollars in. One day and three hours on Saturday or Sunday night.

Without anyone's knowledge two friends and I had purchased an old. Twenty eight model A truck on credit for thirty dollars, that old flat bed that we used to cut. and and haul. Stove wood and sell down in the getto. areas in Atlanta, and when we sold-out of wood and shine we loaded up with produce from the farmers market, and ran door to door selling it until about six in in the afternoon, usually about three truck loads, that was almost three hundred dollars we made on Saturday, about one hundred dollars each, so by Sunday night I had made two hundred fifty dollars most most of it illegally, but but we worked hard at it. Mom thought I was. playing baseball at at the ball park either at our park or in some other other towns nearby. The bank of Prince Albert in the cemetery was full, but not useable for me, I could not spend any.of it for personal use without being found out, and in deep trouble from my dad.

My First venture into the business world was with my friends Charles and Doyle, with the old truck truck we owned, we hauled garbage in my my home town, after school and all day on Saturday, for.fifty cents a barrel. for almost a year, someone in the city govt. evidently, thought we were making too much money, that the city should be getting, so we had to get a permit, we had no Insurance, so no permit, this forced us us out of the garbage hauling business., the citizens demanded the city do what three kids were doing, so they had to buy two garbage trucks and hire four people to operate them, and raised the prices to seven dollars a month, from our fifty cents. That's progress.

So so we went into the stove wood and moonshine, and produce business in Atlanta, with the same truck, and made three times more money than before, that's progress also.

My mom came from a very large family she was number fifteen of sixteen children born born to the Reverend Sam Grimes, he was a very tall man over six foot eleven and for the times considered wealthy, having a large farm and many children to work it, a pillar of the community, and was a leader in the county, known to the governor of the state.as a man to be counted counted on for support.

My My first memories were of of my grandmother Fosters harsh spanking when i was. Three years old back in those days, this happened in Thirty seven, women stayed in bed for nine days after childbirth, it was my brother Troy's birth that she was attending, the baby clothes were being washed outside in November, quite cold that day, in the boiling wash pot, I threw the three severed cat tails, from the young kittens we had out by the wash area that morning, and I was being punished for that. mom thought I was being killed, by the screams I was making, I still remember that, my first introduction to. Pain. The complete wash had to be redone,.my grandmother Foster was dangerous.

School days

My big problem was.me. I. came from.the country, kids were to be. Seen not heard, That's not the way it was in Town, bullying was a new thing to me, and I was was an easy target, never had a fight in in my life, did not know how to defend myself from these wild boys, and I took a lot of bloody beatings in grades three thru grades five, I learned "how to hate" in that period of time, and once puberty started, I ask my dad to teach me to box, my mom was tired of me coming home every day beat beat up and bloody. My clothes torn off, so she encouraged my dad to teach me well, and all the tricks he knew, about a month later I was prepared to go into combat with the bullies, and then it started, they were totally surprised, and I showed no mercy, they had it coming, and I gave it it to them just like they gave it to me for the last two years. I never lost another fight, if you ask for it no matter where we were were you were you got it. School officials and teachers didn't like that, they thought I needed to be conquered by them not. educated an so it went until until my tenth grade, when the teacher in my math class slipped up behind me and slapped me out of my desk on to the floor, She regretted that, because I slapped her back, that got me sent to the principal, he did not find in my favor, then decided to try his hand at punishing me, and I laughed and laughed at him and. Told him to just try it, if you think you can. He didn't try, but he did expelled me permanently, and because. I was not sixteen yet filed charges against me for the incident with the math teacher, and had me placed in the juvenile detention center in Atlanta, that was twenty one days of confinement, known as "cooling it" and I was. I was also wondering why I was here, this was all new to me, Finally my turn with the. Shrink came and I was surprised at some of the questions that he ask me, un believable, things. And thats where I heard heard the word "puberty", and had it explained to me. The judge on recommendation from my school principal, who in the proceedings admitted that he was at thirty six years old, was. Afraid of a hundred forty lb.fifteen year old kid. So I was bared from all schools in Georgia for the remainder of the.school year, "Thank you very much Your Honor., you asshole".

Here I come Camp Hill Alabama, private school, remainder of the. Year. That was a real school, we had a football team, and Basketball team. Back. home we had. Nothing!!!. Unless you count the water fountain in the hall way.

If it had not been for some of my girlfriends who talked to me and advised me wisely to "cool it" it and not to let these kids and teachers get me so mad and upset that I would have lost it sooner, I should have thanked them then they knew it was coming, the teachers made my life miserable for making their life challenging, but they were supposed to be adults. If not for Helen, Ruth, Edna, Charlotte, and Bobbe, school would have been unbearable, then there was my buddy Mayo, he gave me lessons on a few topics that I had missed. They were all part of my good experiences at that school, I finished my schooling at a fantastic high school in. East Point Ga. And have fond memories of those days.

MY SISTER

It was A Sunday am, in forty six when I heard the tires squealing out on the road and the "thump" and lots of loud talking and my mom screaming, I was still in bed I. And my brother ran out on the front porch, and learned that my five year old sister. Sandra, had been struck by a car, she and my little brother. Larry were racing to get the Sunday newspaper for. My dad. The paper box was across the road from the house, she had won the race, got the paper turned and ran back into the road, directly in front of the car, leaving her brother standing In front of the paper box unharmed. She was knocked about 30 feet down the roadway unconscious, the only ambulance available in those days was at the funeral home, she was take to a hospital in Decatur, Ga her Spleen was ruptured, and one leg broken in several places but thankfully alive After many operations and lots of braces on that leg, staples in the bones, to get it to grow back straight, seven or eight years. later she finally got to walk without a brace and no more shots of antibiotics, I know what a mental and financial strain those years cost our family, but. We survived it I was married long before she fully recovered. That was the most tragic thing that affected us as a family until the discovery that dad had mesothelioma and was dying.. In19 64.at the age of 54, my mom had never worked at a paying job and had no skills to do so, it was a tragic situation for the family, there were 3 young boys and one girl still at home at the time, the other three of us were married and had our own family's, I personally lived in Arizona, when my mom called and informed me about my dad's situation, the doctor had told mom he had six months to live, he missed it by one day, dad was gone, I and my family had returned to Ga. Immediately after being notified by mom, Things were hard for mom and money was an issue, so i convinced mom to send one of my brothers out to me in Arizona until he was 18, I taught him a trade, and he has done well since, the others grew up and eventually moved out and mom remarried ten years later, and all's well that ends well, we worked together and prospered.as best best we could under the circumstances.

Grass cutter

One Saturday morning about 6am I had breakfast, didn't get my sponge bath told mom I got grass I promised to cut this morning, gotta go__got my ole push mower tied the sling blade to the handle, hooked up to my bike and away I go.by ten am I had made about a dollar. Time for my bath at the swimming hole its already hot.no one else was there so I peeled off my clothes and dived in, found the ivory soap and washed up, got out on the far side of the pond and laid down on the grass to warm up, the water was a little cool that early. I heard a noise. Off to my right, and jumped to my feet and there just across the barbed wire fence in the woods was a strange girl that I did not know, she looked embarrassed, but I was the one that was naked, but I said hi, she then spoke and ask why I was standing in a cow pasture naked, and at that foolish smart ass moment I told her that I was just "showing off for her, "that made her laugh___ she was about thirteen I guessed, she said that she lived up over the hill with her mom and dad and was from California and was home schooled,, That explained why I had never seen her before my hometown was not that big She kept looking at my "goober" so I put my hand over it, starting at me made me feel naked, and I was.So without any anymore conversation, I moved back toward the pond, and motioned her to follow

Then, smiling at her, I invited her for a swim, she looked back up at. the woods for a moment, and said OK and started undressing, we spent the next two hrs getting very familiar with each others different parts, just playing grab ass mostly, she was as inquisitive as I was, we had a great time almost every Saturday the rest of the summer, Sweetheart wherever you are thank you for the great summer of nineteen forty eight it was great and educational. I learned a lot about girls from you.And you learned a lot about boys from me.and we had a wonderful relationship.and did nothing to be ashamed of, just shared a growing up experience that satisfied our curiosity and expanded our understanding of the opposite sex. It It was A wonderful summer.

A WASTE OF TIME 1949

I ran away from home for two weeks in forty eight hitchhiked from school left with twenty cents in My pocket on a Monday morning and arrived in Oklahoma on Wed.morning about eleven am at my mom's sisters home about forty miles East of Oklahoma City hungry as a bear tired and dirty. my dad had done it again I got suspended from school on Friday for defending myself In A fight with an older kid he kicked me in the seat of my pants walking down the hallway And i jumped him back and was doing pretty good when the teacher showed up that was the third time in a week with the same guy. So I get expelled sent home and he gets to laugh my dad must have had a bad day and a few drinks So naturally it was my fault and I got another one of his best so Monday morning I pretended to go to school and wound up in Oklahoma, Someone ratted me out there and one of my cousins escorted me back home the next week on the big Dog(Greyhound Bus) long. Long ride!!! Plus dad was not happy to see me, and the bus fare just had to come up, Yep Got it again, Next week I was off to Florida got caught in south Ga. I was tired and hungry, Back on the Dog, bus fare came up again. This is not working out at all like I planned, Yep Again, back to school. Same old stuff.. DAMN!!! I just can't get away from here!what to do next?, damn I didn't think it could get any worse but it did, I thought the bus fare was reasonable, too bad I couldn't use my own money to go on these trips.not funny I need a better planner than myself., got to get away. somehow, someway.

THE OLE SWIMMING HOLE AND SNAKES.

When it comes to a swimming hole you have to build a. Dam using whatever is available to get the water deep enough to take a bath in on a hot muggy day in Ga.fifty percent of the boys and girls didn't have indoor bathrooms, that only leaves the swimming hole or a. Lake in the summer it was the place to get clean and much safer than a lake, Ivory soap was our favorite, because it floats, we had rules boys at one end girls at the other, no grab assing allowed, some of them were were a bit shy at first, but soon got over it. Everyone kept the secret, or the parents would have been down at the pool and stopped all our fun, it it was just good clean fun to bathe in the. Pool. And we all got an idea of what what we looked like naked.

SNAKES

We were taught early in life to avoid the serpents found everywhere in Ga.most were not poisonous but. the snake.still was feared by most of us, plus it hurts to get bit by them, I as usual ignored the warnings and got bit three times, my own fault.they were quicker than I was i found out.

The copperhead that that is stepped on was not friendly at all, and was almost the death of me. At the age of five, the other two were harmless except for the pain and explaining why I was stupid enough to get snake bit.Some of my friends at the time thought that was funny.

BAD THINGS THAT JUST HAPPEN

Young marriages in in the thirties usually meant large family's in rural areas the "pill" was mostly just an aspirin tablet held tightly between the knees, and then you have to be able to talk and shout loudly so you can get the attention of the older kids to come inquiring whatever is wrong these tactics seemed to be the favorite birth control methods used for the rural area housewives at that period of time, _many times young married friends would buy land acreage adjoining each other and would help with each other with the farming and other chores, such as out buildings, fencing, timber cutting., Fire wood,. Ect. the result was that as the kids grew up. the concept of I'll trade you my sister for your sister by the boys and the girls also did the same thus any offspring automatically became double first cousins,

In the thirtys transportation was not available for distant relationships with the opposite gender. You needed to be within walking distances or no time to develop a relationship could exist especially if it was to develop to marriage, or to a lasting relationship. that's where "nearer was dearer "term came from. farming was not often one of the safest things a person could do there were many people killed or injured in the homestead areas so a near and dear neighbor was a necessity it was almost impossible for a widow with a family to find a suitable husband in time to save the crops or make ready for the winter unless they had been unusually prosperous in the last few years, little or no money existed, even to move to another location and hope to sell out, in the thirtys barter was the normal way of life. Trade what you had for what you need money was almost non existent. Post Depression was a desperate time to be alive with a large family to feed and care for,.if you had no trade except farming.

The weather was your friend or your worst enemy you either made a good crop or you failed two or three bad weather years and you had to go to chicken farming that's what happened to us in forty Dad went to Atlanta Georgia to find a job after he and his father built a five thousand capacity chicken house in the fall of the year my mom was five twenty five or twenty six and became Chicken Farmers. for the next year or so we just tried to stay alive_and we got our first Batch of baby chicks Dec seventh nineteen forty one Pearl.Harbor Day_That's the day that the world changed and we changed with it, like it or not.it was thrust upon us that day.

My grand father walked to our home that Sunday after church to tell my mom of the declaration of war declared by president Franklin D Roosevelt It was snowing hard that afternoon and I remember hearing my mom crying into the night and I wondered why I was six that year and I had started school early in September while I was only five years old., it was almost six miles to school by the road but only two miles thru the woods_ so dad cut small trees and marked me a path with white barn paint thru those woods to school.and I walked it every day.alone but after a trip in the well bucket down into the well a walk in the woods was a piece of cake even at five years old. And I had no idea what a cotton picking chicken plucker was. Or that I was about to become one.

DARK LAKES AND FROGS

Its sad but true Saturday nights could be a drag back in my teens most of the guys with cars were out with their girlfriends three or four of us "walkers" without cars had nowhere to go and nothing to do, so you go frog gigging at a lake nearby So agreed we head for our gigs and flashlights. At the lake we crawl thru a window in the boathouse because it was locked up and get the alum.boat and two paddles one guy paddles one spots with the light and one handles the gig Everything went fine got 38 frogs in about an hour Until the guy paddling wants to switch with the guy gigging___now the fun starts he gigs a big fat water moccasin snake and sticks it in my face__ so naturally I bail out of the boat in my clothes and shoes, and almost didn't make it to shore I was crying when I got to shore and was I mad both the others were older than I was so a fight was out of the question so revenge is my only option.

I hid in the edge of the woods to think this over they called out to me but I never answered. After several attempts to locate, me one said he's gone home and they decided to go swimming. Pulled off all their clothes and shoes and swam out into the lake

I gathered up all the clothes and shoes and ran with them and threw them in the creek about a mile away I have no idea how they got home naked. But they never ask. me to go frog gigging with them again. And don't know if they ever found their shoes and clothes.

They had some explaining to do at home I bet. I have never liked bullies, I don't tolerate being pushed around or being picked on by anyone, and I always get even, eventually, paybacks are hell, I make sure of it.!! Especially if its personal.!. Practical jokes are exactly that.and are not personal attacks.and to some reason I did not take kindly to the fact that forcing me out of a boat with a snake on a frog gig in my face was not a damn bit funny especially when its fifty or more yards to shore, drowning in a lake at midnight, was not one of the fun things that I was inspired to do at the age of fourteen, evidently they thought it was fun, just like I thought it was fun for them to walk home naked, boys will be boys they say. staying alive alive was important to me at that time in my life.Being naked at 1 am walking home was not exactly life threatening just a lesson in manners. they deserved it.and the fact that they never mentioned it to me afterwards, told me they knew it.I kept quiet about the complete episode telling no one about it.if they wanted anyone to know, let them tell the story themselves.

FIRE. AND A BAD WRECK

Sleeping in the back room at home had its advantages at times, I could climb out the window after everyone else was in bed and not be missed until Sunday am for breakfast.

On one such Saturday night, my two buddy's and a couple of other boys went with me over on a creek to check out the six gallon churn of grape wine I had fermenting over in the swamp, it had the sugar added a few days ago and should be getting ripe but it had not been strained out to remove the seeds and the pulp, So a clean hanky was used and we all had a pint each Wow that was some good stuff!! So we had some more.,!! And Yes we always built a little fire for the light more than anything else, an "Indian" fire we called it the reason for that? Well Indians built. a small fire stood real close white man build big fire stand way back!!

By then it was almost midnight, the Crabapple road bridge over the creek was a short way up stream so we went up and sat on the big wide concrete rails and hatched a plan,_one of their homes was just along the creek we were right next to the driveway to his house and he said that his dad's old model "A" Ford had the engine out of it, Why not push it here push it over cross ways at the edge of the bridge stuff some pine straw into a pair of his dad's overalls lay it beyond the car on the bridge bring the bucket of gas that dad was washing up parts in then wait until we could see a car coming pour out some of the gas on the bridge, and set it afire then run up in the woods and watch. By one am we were ready. About one thirty we saw a car heading towards town about a mile or two away as it got closer the fire was set, The car stopped a man got out looked turned around and went speeding back up the road, we rushed out and removed it all from the bridge and pushed the old car back where it came from swept the fire area with some pine tree limbs and threw sand on the area and waite, its one twenty am before the sirens are heard and the police and fire truck arrived about ten min. Later, We are secure up in the woods watching intently, the police were very upset and voiced their displeasure loud and clear,_poor guy got arrested for doing the right thing, but he was drinking some strong spirits the policeman said.but he got off _turned out he was the judges cousin a minister going home from a prayer meeting as the story was told about town, no one believed that, really.

My hometown In forty nine seemed that if you were related to the "good ole boy" network you could do no wrong, and some of us smart ass kids liked to test that saying at some of the opportunities that we had, and were very familiar with, and we could remain anonymous while doing so, it was fun watching adults squirm, with anticipation, made us feel better, kinda like an Adult Spanking, so to say. Especially if they thought they were more "important" than we were. We. Called it "Comeuppance" and we loved it when they got it!.no one got hurt and we had some fun and a little mischief would keep us boys laughing for a long tim, Another Who done it? the city fathers would like to know because they were aware that someone was on to them. But who? We kids were unimportant and carefree and dumb as a fox. Home towns usually have some things that are not to be spoken of at least in public.

Ice cream in 1940-41

We had some fantastic times in the country, back in forty and forty one Sundays were special that usually meant Company's coming one of my aunts or more would come home from church with us they all had kids!!!!!! Someone to play with!!! Being outside In the Summer in the country was great the peaches were ripe, and mom's sister and family came up from Atlanta and they brought fifty lbs of ice. O. Boy. Ice Tea.!!! And Ice Cream the two best things in the world. My mom mixed up the best peach ice cream mix anyone ever tasted. She used real cream. Me and my cousin went to the peach orchards and got the big really ripe peaches for mom and later after a big dinner had settled the men folks started getting the ice chipped up and the freezer out of the shed and ready to start and the ice cream salt out and in the back yard in the shade,_and then the ice cream making begin it seemed to take forever turning that crank three or four adults sharing in the effort, three hours later about (it seemed)it was done, a big tea glass full of the best ice cream I ever ate was mine. It always took two freezers full to go around, Sometimes it took three,. It was that good, and it only happened two or three times a summer that made it really special mom enjoyed having company, we lived so far from some of her sisters that she grew up with that it was a pleasure to see them and their families I was six years old before I had my first Coke I had a pocket knife, and a watch before my first Coke. Think about that. That shows you how often I went to a store,.of course we had no money and bartering for a coke was a foolish thing to do. My dad sold a bale of cotton that time and felt rich enough to buy me that coke, spent a whole Nickle on me foolishly. What a guy!

1949. THE GOOD OLE. SUMMERTIME JOB

Out of school for the summer, at fifteen _ and dad said I needed a summer job so he got me to apply for one, at an ice cream plant a couple of days later he told me that I got the job, and it was in the ice cream room, That meant I had to get a health card from the health department as a food handler, that means a blood test and a bunch of questions, so about a week later i am on the job, they pasteurized and bottled milk in many different containers, and made all kinds of ice cream and frozen delicacies for kids and adults.so health and cleanliness are a major concern for the employees at that time in Georgia.

I bought my first car in the early that summer of forty nine with my wages I earned, I had been driving without a license for too long (a year or so) in the old truck that we kids had, and was afraid my luck might run out, I got the job working in the ice cream room at the ice cream plant mainly because i was riding with my dad who actually worked for a large truck rental company at the ice cream plant because they leased all their trucks from them and he never missed a day for years, I bought the car from a lady out in Stone Mountain Ga. She and her departed husband had purchased it new and it had been in storage for many years because she didn't drive, I worked with her granddaughter at the ice cream plant so she drove it in for me to see, I loved it and bought it, I had to get my drivers license quick so I listed my age as eighteen rather than fifteen at the time, and took the licence test the next two or three weeks later and it stayed on my record that way until I moved to Az years later. The car turned out to be a thirty three Chrysler four Dr with the sliding glass partition between the front and back seat kinda like a limo which is what I called it. "My limo". Of course all of this had to be on the "Q T" because dad would never have allowed it.

It was a good old car for hundred bucks we boys had a few party's in that one, when you got too drunk to sing, ya have to drive. (Not Really)There was always plenty of mud holes big enough to "anchor in" and keep us safe. The problem was getting out of the mud hole next morning. "Mad Dog" was well named. makes you howl real good tho. I think! we called it singing. Well it sounded good last nite.(who bought this stuff) and all us boys knew every word of every song that Hank Williams ever wrote, and sing at the top of our lungs driving down a country road, it was the thing we loved to do.,

On a rare occasion a girl friend of some of us guys rode around and drank a little Mad Dog with us, if she dared, and helped us out with our singing, most of the girls stayed away from moonshine they didn't like waking up naked and sick it don't get any more embarrassing than that, harmonizing with and some wild crazy country boys and girls on Saturday night, whooping it up! No car was complete without an eight track tape player and some big speakers, and I got them installed at Radio Shack in Buckhead. I think.

All of my rowdy friends liked this also.! Boys will be Boys On Saturday night. And sometimes girls too!!!?the real problem was explaining to my mom and dad whose house I had spent the night with last night or if indeed we had camped out on the river there was no smoky smell on your clothes and where's the fish?and all that mud on your shoes and pants legs, they were quick to see the holes in the story's that were told, I usually let one of my friends drive my car home with him, he did have a legal license to drive, I however was not supposed to own a car not at the time, but soon after I had bought the car I studied the Ga. State driver's license manual about two weeks to be sure I would pass it at age fifteen and I got it

_I did misquote my age about three years but made a perfect score on the driving and written test and was driving my own car, so I was used to how it reacted to my driving style.no mistakes and i was not nervous with it, in fact the Hy, Patrolman that gave me the test even congratulated me on my driving skill, smooth ride he said,.ask me who taught me how, to drive, and whose car this was, I told him it was mine and I taught myself to drive, it up in the country for the last year or so and I wanted to be good when taking the test when the time came to apply for my license.

He said that was smart, and wished everyone did that.and I.Got My License!! I'm legal, well almost..as long as I didn't really screw up something really bad, like a wreck or some other dumb ass thing that would cause a birth record check, (this was back before auto insurance was even thought of) and I never did any thing to receive a citation from the police. So I had wheels! At fifteen look out world! here I come,(as long as dad don't find out) that would be catastrophe and at fifteen would shatter all my plans.__I kept that old car until my "unplanned and unfortunate" trip to the boarding school over in Alabama, That was the year that i had the episode at school that occurred not too long after school started in the fall and i had to wind up in juvi, and then to Alabama for several months.. My car was parked at Ira. Rainwater's car shed, and I had to sell it for spending money while in Alabama.

I got a whopping hundred bucks back for it some times things just don't work out like you plan, I really liked that old Chrysler. and really hated to give it up, but the bank of Prince Albert in the cemetery was far away, and there was no way I was going to get over there or divulge its location to anyone!!.and I needed some money in Alabama, it made life more comfortable over there.plus I had no idea how long I would be there.Far. far from home it was a nice enough place, and it was friendly enough, my first taste of homesickness. And too much time among strangers to think about home.I hated my life, and I hated being a kid. Its got to get better.!!I missed my car, my friends, and my freedom, a boarding school is no place to be, the only reason I stayed there was because of a girl named Sue that liked me, she was there for the same reasons I was, almost, "misery loves company" it was said, and we were both suffering from the "puberty disaster", at home and in school, and in comparing notes we both were in the same situation, she was from Birmingham Alabama, and was just as homesick as I was.

We hung out together a lot, we would at times sneak out at night and walk into town and take in a movie if I had money, we had some almost sex at times I was willing but she was not, and she always won, she never did it, being a virgin was hard decision she had made at about twelve she said and being so lonesome it was a hard one to keep, she needed to be loved she said but not that way, and secretly I agreed with her.Sadly though i don't think she ever had any of her, parents or friends visit her that i remember i think they kinda disowned her i think, I really felt sorry for her, after I was back in Ga., I wrote to her, and one time later the next year I drove over there and visited her, we went out in the back woods and got totally drunk and celebrated our misfortune in life together, in Camp Hill Alabama, what what a complete waste of two darn good kids, Sue and I both, we cried it out that drunk afternoon birds of a feather. Why me, We both wondered.

She had lost her battle with virginity at that time and was still lonesome as ever,. It didn't help at all, it actually made it worse she said, No regular boyfriend. I never saw her again!

Poor girl!I have often wondered if life got any better for her, we were birds of a feather.her family was almost in the same condition as mine, we were a mirror of each other, boy and girl in a hopeless mess, that only time will make better. Everyone at this school I found out later was there for some type of domestic problem or legal problem. Good old Puberty!! wrecking some other kids life. Is this really necessary just To grow up? I wondered, Someone needs to invent a chill pill for this problem, quick.!!.lots of perfectly good kids being thrown away, or hidden out under the pretence of going to a private school, to protect the parents reputation, or as an alternative to reform school, Poor Sue still had two years to go, and I gave her some money and a gross (144) of condoms from the drugstore, and cautioned her about becoming pregnant that it would only add to her problems, she was so homesick and discouraged because her family had not contacted her in almost a year she had written them, but they had moved and left no forwarding address and was so broken hearted, she cried so terribly, and begged me to take her with me when I left.

I was so sorry for her, but where would I take her? I got worlds of problems myself, and I can't ask my aunt and uncle to take in another problem child, I felt so sorry for her.but I was helpless,, I did write her for a long time, and we exchanged thoughts and ideas fo a year or so, her attitude and demeanor had changed a lot in that time, She told me that she loved me and that I was the best friend she had ever had, and that I was right about sex and friendship, and had given away the condoms that I had bought for her to some other girls at the school.along with my messages about them

Sex between a boy and a girl does not, guarantee they are your true friend or ever will be.That friendship ends when the sex does, usually the next day or two, boys move on and the, girls hang on. Very seldom does sex improve a teen relationship, different hormones., different results. Ask anyone who has tried it, the road to ruin is paved with sex stories.some tragic, some heartbreaking. All a great loss of self esteem, puberty at its worst. God what a mess we stupid teens made of ourselves. A little help would have been nice about sex at twelve or thirteen and saved me and Sue from this embarrassing mess Actually a catastrophe with our own selves mentally. I never saw Sue again, and wondered if she made it.

SUMMER. OF. 49

I was on the receiving end of the Popsicles when they were being made in the ice cream room They had traveled thru a twenty five ft long Brine tank inside the mold at a temperature of about minus twenty to become Popsicles with their little stems sticking up my job was to separate them from the mold by pushing the mold down into hot water and pushing down with my thumbs and pulling up with my fingers ___ it worked _ they came out and I placed them on a twin rail rack and pushed them down to the bagging girls, still smoking cold!!

The sticks were released by pushing a little lever as they entered the bagger area the girls were responsible for them now ____ the bags were blown open by air and the weight of them when released caused them to drop into the appropriate paper bags and on to a slow conveyor belt where the girls wearing insulated gloves then boxed them for shipment and shoved them thru the rubber flap into the freezer room. The brine tank was twenty five molds long and twelve molds wide. I had to hurry!!! and remove twelve before the next twelve were pushed down to me, and I had to be careful not to get any of the brine into the molds ruins the taste, it's very salty.and can ruin the complete batch in that mold.

We ran all kinds of ice cream on a stick this way. In different shaped molds When the "sticks" were all run usually by about two thirty pm ___I went to the freezer room at thirty below to help load out the next days delivery trucks until five, pm, quitting time, this is where all the finished products of all ice cream produced by us, came to hardened in here fast. From there it was then loaded out on the route trucks from a pre supplied routing sheet that told us what to shove out on the conveyors that went out of the freezer to the drivers outside who loaded their trucks as they readied them to go to the stores early next am. They were all "plug in freezer trucks" to keep the product frozen and they left out early the next AM some of these guys had long routes to cover. I enjoyed working in the ice cream room but it was only a summer job. but a fun job.! all the ice cream I could eat! Lots of good looking girls to work with and we had some kind of b/s going on all the time what could be more perfect?, Lotta fun and that made the job so much easier, And it paid me good wages for my age and the tax man got his share of this one....boy did he! Jesse James used a gun_Uncle Sam uses a pencil.

Summer 1946 Sex

And now every Teens favorite subject _____ SEX _____ I had heard of it at about eleven but only when it was a mixed crowd with older boys and it always was about "getting some" and that definition implied to me that it was available somewhere in Atlanta, because it was always, see you guys later I'm going to Atlanta to "get some" So my conclusion was that it was not to be had in our town no one ever bragged about it if there was. And as much as was told around the campfire on fishing trips, you would think that the town was overrun with sex crazed young girls just waiting to snatch us young boys up and have their way with us, and we were willing and waiting for that to happen, but sadly it never did.

One of my older friends almost lost two of his teeth in an incident that had something to do with sex one time it seems he went into the local drugstore and bought a "coin pack" and was back out on the sidewalk with a group of us boys, b/s ing with us, when a man rushed up and beat the poor guy almost unconscious I found out later that the man was his local girlfriends Dad, and that the druggist must have called him and reported the fact that he had just purchased three condoms, indicating that a big night was in store for his little daughter because he was known to be her steady boyfriend and daddy was not a happy pappy!!, just the very idea that her boyfriend purchased condoms, set his brain afire.

"A coin pack" is a three pack of condoms. So evidently the druggist was in on this plot So I figured out Sex was also very dangerous as well as hard to find. And the poor guy was on his way to Atlanta that afternoon anyway to "get some" but due to the circumstances didn't make it. So as time passed I and many other boys did not buy coin packs at our local drugstore, that was too dangerous, many of the guys had local girlfriends, but condoms were available in men's public rest rooms everywhere for twenty twenty five cents each in a machine.it was after I was old enough to own a wallet that I as well as most of us carried at least one. Condom in our wallet just in case!!

Got mine at a gas station, But in the late forties there was a great Sex drought that lasted for years _ in and around town__ and our twenty five cent condoms all rotted in our wallets. I think it would have been a wiser idea to have spent that quarter on a milkshake at the drugstore ice cream fountain, I would have enjoyed that, an old rotten condom don't have many bragging rites,__ Sex was kinda like "snipe" hunting non existent. It was several years later that Sex came my way, she was eighteen luckily she knew what to do because I sure as hell didn't, not her way, And it was in Atlanta, at a tennis court and I also learned a condom was not a requirement. At all. She didn't even want to see the one in my wallet_I didn't know how to use it. Properly Anyway, and at two years old it could have been rotten also. about an hour or so later I fully understood why boys went to Atlanta.

Girls in my hometown were not that bold, even in my wildest dreams, she more or less just took control after she found out it was my first time, and gave me a big smile, and the complete Royal 1st class treatment, And that girl really spoiled it for me when I got married. My new wife was not even close to what this girl could do and did!!!. Lack of experience i suppose, Seemed like she was really into it, what a surprise! Wow!!! Finally!!! Happy happy! the boys in town were right. Gotta go to Atlanta to "get some" my town was a dry town. No Sex happening for any Of us boys in this berg Gotta go to Atlanta!!!guys!!! After that experience Atlanta was a new place for us all.

And all that time at the swimming hole with naked girls everywhere _And all the skinny dipping those Saturday and Sunday nights, and all those summer! Mornings with a girl playing in the swimming hole and she was not timid, or shy but, This was not Atlanta She was inquisitive and at thirteen and I guess I fell into that inquisitive category also she was about a month older than I was at the time.and had lived in lots of other places including California

, She had looked at my condom but had no idea what it was used for just like me, I told her it was used for sex but she ask what that was and how do we do it, I don't think I gave her a good explanation, because we didn't try it, I learned a lot from her but that was not one of them, and not all of it was bad or dirty, just the difference between boys and girls down there, we never did anything but look and feel, and touch, she knew how to make it really feel good to a boy and showed me where and how to do the same for her, it was a great way to spend the morning.

Just goofing off with her, no one saw us there and we both had a great time with each other, we talked about lots of things and about lots of places she had lived and interesting things that had happened, and about how much different we were "Down there" and even maybe why we were, she was a very interesting young girl. And I sure did hate to see her go, but her parents got transferred up to Maryland and it was almost time to quit the swimming pool for the fall any way. And I never found another girl like her again, and I missed her, we had a great summer together. It seems I always had to learn everything the hard way Although it may have saved my butt thinking of some of the guys experiences.

Small towns have some unwritten Rules that unfortunately were not passed around to us pee_wees!.Everyone looks out for everyone else in those days.Hard way to learn boys!!!Hard way to learn!!!But being ignorant of a lot of things kept some of us boys safer, so we were not in too much danger because being young and not overly interested in sex at this age we got off easier than some of the older ones.

THE THE ART OF BEING DUMB

"Dumb" may have saved our skinny little butts, because some of those parents were Real dangerous and messing with the local girls was the same as a death sentence.!!! Dumb was better than being too nosey when it comes to Girls.Especially small town Girls they were as dumb as we boys were when it came to how to and when to and where to. Ya gotta go someplace where these things were happening, big boys say you got to go to Atlanta now that's a different place and different girls, they were much bolder and older and seemed to know things I had never even thought of, and à lot of _Strange things were told to us pee wees that were downright kinda scary by some of the boys story's that the older boys told that were known to have had experienced a few trips into that area in Atlanta, But that vital information as to where in Atlanta to go was not divulged.

And What happen there, "supposedly"!! We were told. But often some unexpected things really did happened at times, as I found out a few years later We were so Country.and so dumb Like we just fell off the turnip truck! this morning, when it came to the subject of sex its amazing what a thirteen year old boy will believe!!!.its hard to stretch my imagination now, about what goes on in our adolescent minds about some of things that puberty sings to us., and sad that its all wrong and so confusing. Being a kid is really hard.from ten to sixteen so much to learn and experience to believe.Boys and Girls and so little time.

SUMMERTIME & HOME IN 1950

OUTTA school summertime, got permission to go back home In fifty, my probation officer thought it would be a chance to see if things were improving between my Dad and I so I arrived on the next Sunday, For A two or three week visit to my mom and dad, They had moved back to the country months ago and mom had just sold her birds on Monday. big chicken roundup, time catch them, coop them, weigh them, and load them.And Thursday mom got paid And I had twenty bucks In my jeans for helping out for a couple of days, Happy days, hitchhiked to Buckhead (north Atlanta) to go to a movie I wanted to see went to the pool hall for another lesson in how to waste my money betting at fifty cents a game, left the pool hall with a pint of Peach and Honey @100 proof_and that proved to be one of my most memorable occurrences,, I do remember drinking some of it, not all of it, but Don't remember how or who took me home about two am about thirty four miles north of where I was.at the time. I remember some of the fight with my dad, that night, but not much else.

Afterward my mom filled in the blanks a few days later She said it lasted about an hour, and it started when I began telling my dad off about how he had abused us kids, and how tired of his crap I was, and I was not taking it anymore,. it must have been a real nasty mess though because Sunday morning about ten am dad came into my bedroom and said Rather loudly GET UP!! I was not prepared for how I felt as I tried to do that _even my toe nails hurt! Mom handed me a cup of coffee and two aspirin as I entered the kitchen, i must have looked as bad as i felt, dad said "get in the truck" O boy now I know he is going to take me off somewhere and kill me for sure! We drove up the road a ways and he turned on to a little used road and about two mins. Later stopped and said "get out" O God!!! This is it!!!I thought "come on" he said and headed into the woods now I am petrified, but I followed he walked up to a brush pile threw off a few limbs and there in the shade was a big tub of Beer in ice and water so evidently he had put there the afternoon before, so we carried it back to the truck poured off the water and put it in the bed of the truck then he opened one and handed it to me saying with a chuckle "look like you could use this" I almost melted, that was the best Beer I ever had_ at the best time in the best place from the best guy. In world right now, I was hurting, bad, real bad, but i was not going to admit it to him, that's a fact.

We then went to one of my uncles and we all went fishing up on a lake had two more Beers before going home, and we had fish for supper. I went to bed early not even dark yet. The episode was never mentioned again. And the next week after the chicken house had dried out I was still a little sore in places as mom and I started shoveling chicken manure from the houses to the old wagon to haul it away to the corn field. "Much to learn yet young squirt" my mom said.__Yes indeed. I thought. Yes Indeed! And after that, my dad and I had a different relationship from then on mom said we both needed and got an attitude adjustment.

That I had did pretty darn good and stood up for myself against my dad even if I was a little "tipsy" and then she gave me a little peck on the cheek, whatever it was for for it don't know but, that I did, it worked. He and I became a lot more friendly with each other, and even agreed on some things._ mom said we were just alike.Dad didn't look to good with all those bruises and black and blue spots all over his body mom said he wasn't as young as. he thought he was, and laughed.i think she enjoyed seeing dad catching a few hard licks, she seemed amused, about the whole thing.

Stubborn and Bullheaded, I think she was right. For the first time in a long time I enjoyed being home and helping my mom with the birds it was hard work cleaning out those houses, and getting them ready for a new batch of baby chicks, and mom was tired that summer and was glad I could to come home and help, it was awfully hot that summer and some of the birds were almost grown and hungry so we gave them extra food and water. Catching twenty twenty five thousand chickens by hand is hot stinky, dusty work and requires two full days to accomplish even with lots of help but it's gotta be done.and somebody's got to do it or you don't get paid.and that's why they did it I truly don't know how my mom kept going, my brother was thirteen then and was working with mom and he was a big strong boy (grew up to be 6_ft 3) then there was, a full house of kids, seven in all Including myself_ nice family, love them all. But still too young to be a lot of help to mom, but they all worked together and they made it, I felt bad that I could not be there to help, but with the circumstances that were in control of my life at the time it was not a favorable consideration, I had a problem getting to come up for the two or three weeks, they were trying to keep my dad and i apart, but mom needed help with all of the birds she had, but at least they were at different ages which was a good thing, the small ones needed less food and water, and their houses kept a little warmer even in the summer otherwise she would never make it alone, or she would have had to cut back on the numbers of birds she cared for, at least there was not any cotton to pick. Later in the fall, that's hard work after raising chickens all summer, with little time for rest and recovery.

And I could only stay for twenty days. Max. i was told. What a mess!!! I sure had one helluva a hard time growing up.!!But at least I was getting a decent education at my new high school and a lot of exercise up at the chicken ranch.But I was young and strong, and it was a good feeling to see my family for a change, I think I missed them more than I realized, it was a good three weeks.and nice to be back with my aunt and uncle and no turmoil.But what was real?and what was normal?_ I really didn't know. One Day at a time I decided.!

More adjustments needed 1951

I had applied for a job at The ice cream place, again and had to go for my interview on Wed, I wanted to drive a special little truck called a T G route truck, on the street ice cream sales truck. it was a fun job and an opportunity to meet with all types and races of people, exciting changes coming in my life.as I gained some real world experience, some was a little more than I had ever encountered but I remembered what my mom always said, "can't never could do nothing" so I jumped in and tried and some how some way managed to be good at it eventually. No matter what it was try it you might like it, some of it I did, sometimes I didn't. But I tried, and that's what experience is all about. Live and learn in action. Very satisfying to a teenager to feel accomplishment, no matter what the task. I guess I was beginning to feel the first pangs of growing up.____ About time I thought and I really had a different attitude about a lot of things after seeing what all this was doing to my mom, and how much older she looked since I had been gone from home.But I'm glad now that dad and I are on better terms, I'm tired of being a kid, How long does puberty last I wondered, is this what I'm supposed to feel? I think I know, but do I?.really? This new body's brain was having some problems and some more adjustments were needed!!.

Back in high school 1951

The new High School was everything that my old stomping grounds back in the home town was not, it was not possible to go to school for two terms and not be accosted by some guy or someone about something, but I did. I was almost in shock, I never heard a teacher raise his or her voice to a student and if someone didn't understand something you were not passed up __ it was explained three or more times in different ways and then with student participation until you got it, these people were pros. And the kids were helpful also. Study hall was a study hall not a free for all. It took me quite a while to believe this was real..and in study hall even the students helped if. You were having a problem with any particular subject another student would pair up with you to help yo wow this was great. Unbelievable but great.

One particular girl in my home room really got my interest big time, I had student tokens to ride the Trolleys from College Park to the school in East point For those who don't know what a trolley is its an electric powered bus that requires two wires overhead in the street and two poles in back of the bus going up to the wires and the trolley is equipped with rubber tires and rides very good and very quiet, but I really wanted to walk so I could spend more time with her she also had tokens for the Trolleys. and she wanted to walk with me also, So after the first semester we were a couple, I had to explain to my Aunt why I was so late getting home at times but she smiled and said she understood, and ask me to bring her home with me anytime to meet her, and after a note to her mother a day was arranged for them to meet. My Aunt hardily approved of my choice of girlfriend and told her so.it was the. beginning. of a relationship that I never wanted to end this was not like anything I had ever felt before. What's happening to me? Very confusing.

My senior year we had a sock hop and had a live band play that night_ in East Point it was Jerry Reed The "Alabama wild man" that became a Movie Star with Burt Reynolds. What a wonderful night I had with Pat, we spent a lot of time that night after the dance sitting down in the little park just past her house lots of the "mushy stuff" that boys and girls do when no one's looking..took place. It was an awfully bad spot for me I was so crazy about this girl, but I had tons of skeletons in my close I really wanted to tell her that I was still on probation from the juvenile court system, and why, but I froze up, that was just too hard and embarrassing to explain to a girl like her, She could not possibly understand.I didn't understand myself at times why and how there was so much turmoil in my life, does this happen to everyone?how can I explain it to her, I don't really understand why I'm like this, I didn't want to be, and I was so happy with Pat and my progress I didn't the new high school.

I had to report every month and bring my report card in to my "shrink" at the Juvi. center I now know how some of these men feel getting out of prison. I just did not know how to tell this girl that I was a real zero without taking a chance of losing her or that her parents would get involved, if it came to that they would certainly insist that she associate with someone else with a better reputation than I had.Or that we were going to be criticized so badly to get us broken up someway, I think it was my first time in my life of feeling so ashamed of myself. For my past. I wanted to stay and I wanted to run. I didn't want to ruin her life. I cared very deeply for my girlfriend And I was sure she felt the same for me. So I ran.I went away That was the hardest decision that this country boy had ever made and the easiest dumbest solution that I could have made, selfish is what it was. Because the day I entered the military my probation dropped. Gone!! Over!!! Done!!

But I also lost her It was three years later that I accidentally met up with her. In a department store in Atlanta, And we both were married. Too late now!!! But that old feeling was still there. Both of us. We Still felt it, she started crying and I tried to apologize, but how could I ever defend my stupidity to this girl_Not the fairy tale ending this time!.I cried most of the way home!!!! That was a Hurt I had never felt!. I never saw her again, I can only hope that she forgave me. for my stupidity, I really loved that girl!

I met another girl at a soda fountain not far from my uncle's home out in College Park Georgia.

And she lived with her mother and brother her parents were divorced she went to school in the adjacent community she was a good looking blonde girl but a little strange I didn't know why I felt that way about her she was also sixteen at the time I later learned she also was on probation out of Juvi. When we met at the same probation office downtown Atlanta.one Saturday morning at juvi. Her offence was shoplifting, clothes to wear to school, seems her father and mother divorced and he had. Remarried and her mother didn't make enough money to support the three of them. Did that sound familiar to me? I genuinely felt for her, Seems like the world was full of silent misery everywhere I turned, I was not the only one with problems. So we dated a few times. this was about the time that I had met my steady girlfriend Seems Misery loves company also, they say,_Things were fine for a little while, we were in different schools hers was NOT like mine and I was able to help her some with that, but one Sunday night we went to her church together and we went to the rear entrance of it and back in there in the trees up on the steps she started kissing and fondling me sexually and after a short period of that offered me sex for ten dollars.wow. was Was I surprised!!!

To say I was shocked is putting it mildly, never in my life had this happened to me, I didn't have ten dollars damn it all. I most likely would have paid it at that "Time" I lost interest in her promptly, after that discussion, wow!lot of my respect for her vanished quickly, it was only about the money, but then.I also found out later that her brother was in with her,_he brought her some of his friends that had ten dollars he was three years older, poverty boredom Too much need_ not enough money, Bad combination.

Nice girl, bad brother, bad situation,.poor girl the deck was already stacked against her_I have wondered many times if she made it.I sure hope so, I wanted no part of this, and I really felt genuinely sorry for her,, how can a brother do this to his sister? I got lucky, I did., With some good help, and a lot of patience from the right people and attitude. And I thought back to the times when I used my dads pickup truck to make some money tripping moonshine, to make money, poor girl didn't have a pickup, she was using her body to do the same thing I did.

God what a mess we make out of ourselves. Poverty drives some of us to some extreme measures when we are young.and want so much. Puberty and a out of control sexual appetite is a terrible thing for a girl her age, and no parent to guide her and a terrible brother.That alone is a large influence that others more fortunate don't have.. And we the less fortunate strive so desperately to ignore and can't, Its maddening at times, now add puberty, and a large dose of pride to the equation and there stands me.!_I was beginning to understand.my lot in life. And I didn't like what I saw.compared to her problems, mine were minor.! I had a long talk with her later but it was too late she admitted that she really enjoyed the sexual encounters and wished for more, and that her brother, often had sex with her at her request.Too late she was lost.and that's one time I was glad that I was not a girl. Damn. that was really a big trap to ever break out of for a even break in life she was going to need a lot of luck. I hope she got it.I moved on with Pat, she was a real down down to earth girl.

Fire drills

I had a lot of relatives on my mom's side of the family when I was growing up in my teens and my pre teens I got to see and visit most of them, and there was about 40 or so cousins on mom's side but on my dad's side not so many about seven or eight cousins and. only a few visits, per year moms crew were all the visiting kind, they had to be there were eleven family's so everywhere you went some one else was there, also and mom always generally decided where to go, its probably a good thing she could not drive a car she would have been gone most of the time, and I would have had to raise all those chickens by myself. It was like a Chinese fire drill on Some weekends.I always liked for all them to come to our house I was always more comfortable at home than when visiting, my dad only had one sister and she was a favorite of mine, it was quiet and peacefully at her house and she would talk to us instead of shooing us outside to play I always liked that it was nice to visit her its like we were a person also, she reminded me of her father, they both spoke softly to you so you had to pay attention to what she said to hear her.

I can't remember hearing her raise her voice to any of us or her children, and even after I became an adult and lived out in Arizona she was always high on my list to see before leaving.for home.One of the most gracious persons I've been privileged to know in my life my Aunt Played the piano at Church for almost as long as I can remember, Now after almost a 100 years on loan to us she has gone home. But she left us all that marvelous talent with the piano with her daughter.

She has carried it toward to new and modern levels to the pleasure of thousands of people that have heard her play the piano, what a fantastic gift, the gift of music.To soothe the savage beast in all of us.and give us hope for the future, I have wished many times that I.had been blessed with that talent but it was not to be, even if I bought myself myself a beautiful Gibson J45 guitar, and spent hours trying to play it, but I never had the musical talent to do it. I can do many things, that others can't do but that J45 Gibson Gibson has escaped me.

Promises I made to myself 1951

Each of us in our own time learn the lessons of life in pretty much our own way and it takes time to mature and it takes patience, and for a fifteen year old it takes forever!!! Yes I still remember in this age that I am today that those were some very short years. That I made into long ones, and I'm sure that I'm not the first to note that.

Definitely after I learned the value of "Money" there was nothing that was too much work, or too much trouble, to make it for me, i had the means the energy and the scheme's to accomplish all of this and to make it happen it seems there was never enough of it in our family either, we were always in want, or need of something, and I was on that list also.

As I grew in age and determination, I learned the hard way that making and having money was two different things, I made some, not entirely legal, and because of that I was not able to use it as I wished, so having it was entirely useless, a very complicated mess that I had created because of it, and.after I got into the ice cream business I gave away some to the poor that I had no problem feeling sorry for, and spent some of my commission making up the shortages that were created, after my teenage life, I always pull for the underdog, we have so many of them in today's world., And from all the trouble and deprivation that I had in my day, I still managed to hold onto enough of my Christian upbringing to survive, and now feel that my moms and others prayers did in some way affect my life to make it better, and I can assure you that I had to make some major adjustments, to my life that at the time I did not favor, but I did them,_Its called growing up_some of us bask in the glory of it successfully and some of us fight it tooth and nail dismally.

But like the Sun Rise every morning It is going to happen, it Comes to each of us at some age._Its part of the Cycle Of Life, Wish I had realized that back then.!I still carry some of the scars from that needless battle.. But I also know that as bad as I thought mine was there are some who self destruct like the poor girl that I had known back when I was in high school with the pervert brother and the unaware mother, I don't think I had ever realized that I was so wrapped up in my own personal web of troubles to not feel the. Pain of others.

Realized that perhaps things could be terribly wrong for other kids my age that i was not aware of, and that just to end the mental torture of puberty, its a good thing I was also stubborn as a mule, and had a fiery temper to match.but I had learned that it was not really all about me, there were many others that were as bad or worse than my circumstance was to me, and nothing that I could do about it and it made me sad to think what others were going thru at the same time I was, and I was troubled,

I refused to surrender. And with all that, there were times when i was in deep trouble that it crept into my mind.but I didn't dwell on it. And focused my thoughts on some girl that meant a lot to me and that made me smile, and my life didn't seem so bad anymore.

A little selfish I suppose, but I had finally realized that it was not always going to be like this, so I resigned myself to never forget what I am seeing and feeling at this point in my life, and someday that I would try to make a difference somehow, some way.for those going thru the confusing years that puberty brings upon us, and to the parents.

We don't understand an adult's concerns, and some parents don't understand adolescents behavior and concerns, believe me a lot of us are scared and confused and at times unpredictable. And that means big trouble for all involved.we don't plan it, it just happens.a failure has occurred and its always the adolescents fault?? That is the effect, now what was the cause??think about that mom and Dad, could it have been prevented? How?

Tornado Time! 1938

Dad was working in Atlanta after the spring crops was planted on the farm up in the country and had went back to Atlanta before he lost that job, that in turn left my mother and i to finish with the garden and the traditional spring cleaning of. the household, We were all alone back in the sticks. Back in the late Thirties, my mom and I had to stay alert in the summer, we usually had some storms that were scary but at times were terrifying to a woman and a small child, we needed the rain for our crops but tornadoes, or the possibility of them were a constant threat, also at that time of the year, mom always kept an eye to the sky so we didn't get caught out in the field too far from our storm shelter, it was a hand dug area that dad and mom also helped dig out over the first year that that dad had bought the farm, those things were literally a necessary item to have out in the area we.were in, It Was in the backyard behind the smoke house, it was a long trench that kept getting deeper into a small hill side then terminated in a large room that was underground and had benches carved in the walls to sit on, that were covered with old used oil cloth(used to cover the kitchen table as a table cloth). They were water proof so if mom said run to the storm shelter quick!! I ran We had an old kerosene lantern hanging from the ceiling and some matches in there for light because it was very dark in there when the door was shut. There were in our area several tornados that struck, but we were always spared thankfully However once we were at my grandfathers one Sunday after church (moms dad) and we had left for home after dinner in dads mule drawn wagon, not quite half way home, when a sudden very dark cloud began to gather, and it got very dark and the wind was getting very strong, and my dad pulled into someone's yard that they knew an mom and I ran to the door and knocked, we went inside as dad unhitched the mule and tied him to a 4x4 at the well shelter and ran into the house also, mom took me into the back bedroom and made me crawl under the bed as a terrible Roar came thru and loud thumps and wind whistles shook the whole house, mom was crying and dad was down on the floor hugging her, then the noises went away. just as suddenly as they came, and it was very still and quiet, with an Eerie green colored sky, and everyone was praying aloud for God's protection, After a few more minutes dad and all of us went out on the front porch, only to to see that the man's Barn and sheds on the barn were completely gone.Blown away!!! His mule and cow were also gone, my dads mule was still tied to the well shelter and his wagon was still as he had left it, about 25 yards from the missing barn, we were extremely fortunate, that day, and that was something that left a very strong impression on me at 4 years old. A few weeks later there was a barn raising for them and everyone in the area was there. To rebuild what was lost, I remember spending the night there, and others also i don't know about the mule or the cow that was lost, I would guess that someone donated replacements for those also, And i think that a storm cellar was dug for them out in the backyard also, Good neighbors were the norm back then.

Years later 1946

Years later in 46 in my hometown I had ridden my bike hard to escape the coming storm one afternoon after school, just barely made it into the house as the wind and a whipping rain hit, I grabbed a piece of sweet potato pie from the table and went into the living room to do my homework and had only gotten about ten minutes into it when the whole complete window next to my chair was sucked right out of the house, Whoosh__ it and the one in mom and dad's bedroom just went away also!!Gone along with all my homework that I had just completed, now I know my teacher is not going to believe this! _Because I'm having a problem believing this myself, mom came running into the room from the kitchen asking what on earth was that?

We now have two very large holes in the east side of our house where windows once were, and that we need to cover and nail those holes shut because it is raining like crazy and this needs to be done quickly before dark if possible.. Mom called dad at work and he brought four sheets of plywood and some nails home as soon as possible and we did it before dark, and we were all drenched in the rain.Dad said that the "Twister" passed up high over the house and created a vortex that pulled our windows out, much lower and the roof and house could have been destroyed. But it was a month or so before the windows were bought and installed, money was the problem with that, a window complete with glass in the size we needed was about fifty five dollars.

We had no insurance on the house, and dad only made about forty five per week, one of my first cousins was building his first house on the new road over behind our house and I'm almost sure that he bought them for dad with some of the proceeds from his FHA loan, to build his new house, and then because I was loaned out for the summer to help them build three of them before winter that year, I don't know if Dad or I worked that debt out with him. That information was none of my business I was told. But I did receive a Hearty Thank You from the guys.for my help that summer and fall, no money, just Thanks!.

But just look at the experience I had gained at driving nails, and sawing wood!! It wasn't every day, some days they didn't need me, it depended on what was being done that day.I got pretty good at driving nails at twelve years old.and that fact came in handy when I built my rabbit boxes later that fall with some help from mom and the use of the wood scraps and nails from the construction of the homes we built plus they had given me my very own saw, and hammer and a carpenter apron, pencil, and folding ruler, I was in tall cotton big time. Ready to build something, Carpenter!!! At twelve years old in forty six and I was a proud little guy of my tools that they had presented to me, it was a happy moment for me to feel appreciated by my cousin and his friends. even if the tools were old and used they were mine.mine mine!

Crayfish - Crawfish 1948

Hunting and fishing were big time items for my age group when the water in the creek got too cold to play in, and the girls quit showing up at the hole. Craw fish were fairly common in the creeks all over the area that I lived in (craw fish are basically freshwater shrimp)and my mom really knew how to prepare them, but they were quite wary of us kids, I eventually made me a small net just for them and a big Maxwell House coffee can full was a rare treat that dad even showed partiality to them.

Mom made them with rice and some other herbs with some hot peppers mixed in boy o boy were those good, and the fish we caught in the creek were so full of bones and not really big enough, but we tried the real big ones were down in the Big River and it was too dangerous for us 12 year old guys to go there we would have to wait to get older and maybe the fish would just get bigger and wait for us to catch them and they did and we did, catch them that is, and those big Channel Cats were some good eating, I never caught one of the fifty pounders but have seen them. My big one was about twenty lbs. And that one scared my mom, and she was upset with me for going there and chastised me severely, even tho I was now a full fourteen years old, but did partake in the spoils. and made some great tasting _Hush puppies with it., Dad was too busy eating to comment. That one I got away with!. glad he did not ask anyone where that big ole fish came from. It would have been terrible to got a whipping after eating and enjoying that meal.

Carp Fishing 1948

In the spring in Georgia it rains and then it rains some more, back before the flood control dams were built on the big Chattahoochee River it would flood all alongside both sides of the river and as it receded left large ponds of water filled with fish avoiding the torrent of the flow, and got trapped in these ponds of still water next to the dirt road alongside alongside the river, and in another two or three days they would die from lack of water, so it was get them or let them go to waste, and it also meant playing hooky from school to go down there and use pitchforks to get these big fish, the majority of them were very large Carp up to ten lbs, and some were catfish, because they don't bite a hook when trapped like this, plus lots of people don't or won't eat a trash fish like Carp, but if you know how to prepare the Carp they are not only eatable but also delicious, I hate to keep saying this but my mom sure knew how to make fish patties from the Carp that were fantastically delicious, she made them like salmon patties and they were a hit when she made them for us, the problem I had was, explaining how I came by twenty five lbs of fresh Carp and a few nice sized catfish at four in in afternoon after being in school all day,? That was problematic as far as my mom was concerned, she didn't just fall off the turnip truck either. Sorry mom I think I got a ball game to play in this afternoon that I almost forgot about, and I've got to run, catch you later mom!bye, grab my ball bat and run quickly before I have lie my butt off to my grinning mom. She knew how and where I I got them. Dad will love supper tonight, she's thinking.

Can you see now how I stayed in at least as much trouble as Tom Sawyer, and Huck Finn back in those days I fear that I was closely following in their footsteps without realizing it. Poor mom, separating fact from fiction with two boys was a tough job,. I think she had most of it figured out but, we were not hurting anyone but ourselves and we were Boys__Growing Boys. And I guess our hearts were in the right place, bringing home the fish for the family, it seemed important to us but going to school was important, to us and our parents, and we were short on food at times so who Was right and who was wrong? Mom just let it lie where it was and did not mention it to dad, she knew what would happen if she told him where the fish came from,. And the funny thing was that he never ask where they came from, But I got the warning that Next Time Young Man!!There will be a price to pay. fortunately the floods only came in the spring and usually were not too severe, as to flood the area too badly, it had to be a serious flood for the fishing to be really good, and we still did the same thing with the same results..Poor mom.

After I grew up and moved out of my hometown I ask mom one time why she stuck up for us back in those days, And her answer was "Your dad never brought home any fish" only empty bottles, and come to think of it She was right!. He never ask where they came from., and she didn't tell him.But if he had known that I brought them home, all hell would have broke loose! guess they just floated in the back door, I never ever quite fully understood my Dad. And I don't think my mom did either. But he was the "man of the house".. And that was the Accepted Traditional way family's were run.in the South. Any disagreement was not for our ears, and any questions that came up between the two of them stayed between them we were not privy to that and it was not aired in front of us kids, but in private, and confidential terms. That was also the Traditional methods of Mothers!!!. No one in my family doubted for one second about mom.

The influence that mom possessed on any subject!!!.mom was. cool and could really make my life great when she wanted to, and also the other way if necessary.if food was involved, mom usually smiled thru almost any elaborated tale we kids came up with without any problems with the story..

Getting ready in 1947

The dogwood trees were in full bloom and the air was getting warmer and spring was in the air, and this is the time for a young man's fancy to turn to love, but at this house it was time to start to cleaning out the chicken houses, and no one loved that, mom had decided not to raise any during the winter because the last batch had not been as profitable as they should have been and when you added the extra cost of coal to heat the houses it would not pay, so when the last ones sold they were not replaced, and that left the houses in need of cleaning out and new window curtains also, so lots of work was required to restart the houses into condition to receive a new batch of little baby chicks in the spring, but just because we were ready to get going again did not necessarily mean that everyone involved was ready, willing and able, there were others involved.And we all had to pitch in and get things moving and, mom had to sew up new window curtains or window coverings as some were called, a few small leaks in the tin roof needed some tar to correct that plus the old shavings and manure had to be cleaned out and hauled away to the fields this meant using the mule and wagon.

The Mule Wreck 1947

You could bet that when the mule had not been harnessed up and been in the traces for pulling the wagon since late last fall she was going to be reluctant to go back to work this spring, and would be stubborn about getting caught, if she had room to run, because if you had a halter or a bridle in your hand she was aware of what was in store for her and run she did, so my brother Troy and I tried to chase her back into the barn for an hour or more without luck, so we locked the barn door and didn't feed her for two days, She was more cooperative when the door was opened this time, so while eating, I slipped into the stall and put on the halter, then led her out to the wagon and hitched her up to it went over to the chicken house we were cleaning out and loaded the wagon, and started to the field to unload, when ole Kate decides to run a little as soon as we got to level ground, and after a few minutes showed no sign of slowing or stopping as I was pulling on the reins she was determined to run, so my over enthusiastic brother whacks her across the rump with a big wide shovel and made her go faster now we got a stupid runaway, mule and just about the time I think she is going to stop whacks her again even when she wants to stop she gets whacked again, I can't control the mule and my brother both, I never had this happen before so finally I decided to just hang on one of them has to stop sooner or later in the process the mule kept going off to the right on the roads soon we are approaching the road back home after making a huge circle and, with the bumpy rough ride we have lost almost all of the load of manure, it has bounced out of the wagon, now the mule makes a tight right turn onto the road to home.

The wagon overturns throwing me and my brother out, there was a barbed wire three strand fence there, I went over the fence the wagon was on the fence the mule was in the fence with my brother, I landed on my left side and arm, and was hurt, my bro was hanging upside down on the fence and was choking on his coat collar that was hung up in the barbed wire the mule was kicking and bleeding from a gash torn in her left front shoulder.

I'm yelling for help!!! Mom heard and came running and saved my brother from strangulation in the wire, and together we finally got the wagon over on its wheels and the mule unhitched from the wagon and then out of the wire, by then some of the neighbors had arrived and were helping untangle the barbed wire mess What a wreck!!! After that debacle my brother walked up the hill to the field or rode at the rear to unload the wagon, from then on. We had no choice but to continue because mom had baby chicks coming in 4 days and this mess had to be done and ready to receive them.by then I think that was back in the spring of forty seven_before I was thirteen in the fall.

I can't remember exactly, but it was a learning lesson for all of us, and the poor mule had to work injured just like the rest of us, it was a close call for us, we were not ready for the chicks, luckily some one from the hatchery over in Woodstock came by and told mom that they were going to be a couple of days late on the delivery which saved us.and we were ready for the little yellow guys when they arrived._ and Troy, he didn't spank the mule with a shovel ever again!!! Poor mom with all this adolescent help, its amazing anything got done correctly, But you gotta work with what you got, looking back now, how many young boys at nine and twelve years old could handle a mule and a task like that today? Mom depended on us to get it done, and we were a little late and bruised up, but we did it.!! And that was all that mattered that time.it was miraculous that things worked as well as they did, with the help mom had with only us kids as her partner's.but she knew how to get us to do our best to please her, we worked very hard for mom!!! Because if we didn't do it she would, because it had to be done, rain or shine.

Beer drinking dog 1951

Mushrooms are all over the place in the woods, by the creeks, in the garden, in the cow pies in the pasture, but I was always afraid to eat wild rooms, I have heard that some are extremely deadly and there are experts that won't and can't eat some of them so how do you know which is which?well my buddy Tom had a dog that loved Beer, _yep Cold beer so after a beer he would eat mushrooms if they were boiled in butter and beer if the dog threw them up, Don't eat those if he wanted more, those were OK.

Tom and the dog were pretty convincing with this so called proof of safety thing, but my Stomach and my brain were not in tune with his Dogs stomach, as far as I was concerned were not the same in comparison to what may or may not digest. In the mushroom family So I stuck with what I know as far as mushrooms are concerned, but Tom was not swayed in his logical interpretation of his theory, So one afternoon I went by the Funeral home to pay my respects to Tom and his dog and there on his chest was that mushroom tee shirt that he loved, Sorry old friend but is it possible the dog was wrong? I think so! Playing with mushrooms to me is like playing Russian Roulette with only one bullet.one out of six is not good enough odds for this country boy!!!a thousand to one odds won't work with those mushrooms for me either, and I love mushrooms.and I ate many a variety of them but somehow i just didn't trust my life to a beer drinking dog! Would you?

Dads 46 Chevy in 49-50

Its not that my dad didn't understand progress, and in the Automobile world there was quite a lot of it but he was pretty well as the old country people said "Sot" in his ways, back during the WWtwo thing he always had Chevrolets, and I was not old enough or experienced enough to even have an opinion about those things, and when learning to drive, well that was an antique that we three boys had in that old twenty eight Ford flatbed model A that we used to haul everything with, and dad did have a fifty Ford pickup that I was privileged to drive upon occasion's and made a Lotta money with, but he always wound up somehow back into another Chevy, and after I got a little older and more daring behind the steering wheel those old Chevy's just were not tough enough to be able to handle my large foot and small brain, and he could drive those things for months with nothing breaking, and I could only drive them minutes and seems everything broke, and seven cases of half gallon jugs was a full load of "Shine" in those things and you know it can't break when on a run, that can lead to disaster,

I learned to replace axle's on the side of the road drop the oil pan and tighten the Rods and you got to carry at least a gallon of motor oil in the trunk just in case, The worst possible disaster was to have the top of a piston come off and float inside the cylinder of the block, that was tow rope time, and it never fixed the car but beating my ass seemed to help.in the repair process for dad, I bought Chryslers, Dodges, and Desotos, evidently I was just too young to drive his car, or the darn thing just didn't like me, because it usually broke something if I Was driving it even if dad was riding with me, I hated that old green thing!!!I had a beautiful old Plymouth that I had completely rebuilt end to end, I gave it to dad, because his old clunker had fell apart, and what does he do?

Yep. ___ drove it down to the Chevy Dealer and traded it for another Chevy Soon as I found out where the Plymouth was I went to the Dealer and bought it back from them. That really ticked me off, and to top that off I had to hide it from him, because I was supposed to be broke, no money!!!!!Sometimes after I got used to having made money I kept it on me instead of in the cemetery tin can. And I almost got caught a few times like that time.I got careless.sometimes, but never got into anything I couldn't get out of.thankfully..

Girls 1939---1942

No matter how hard I tried I always wound up stuck on some girl in school it started in the first grade, there was one that just would not let me alone she followed me everywhere except the boys room, however if we were playing in the trees or the woods she always had her hand in my overalls and led me around by the yang_ yang,.molesting me at an early age.

It was a habit she would not break any time we were alone she managed to get me, I was too young to be embarrassed by it and didn't know at that time that it was not proper for young girls to do that and I don't remember the teacher talking to either one of us about that so it went on for two terms of school mostly at recess before we moved to the burbs in forty two then it was the girl next door that molested me all the time in her playhouse in the woods but she had three brothers older than her and she told me she did it to them all the time.

And there was three of my first cousins that I was afraid of, they were always carrying me off to the barn loft or out under the grapevines and groping me all the time and kissing me like maniacs, I hated to go to visit some of them I used every excuse I could come up with not to go, then at about fourteen I got even with them, the shoe was on the other foot it was my turn to grope and tweak them for a change puberty was my friend now!! I didn't realize girls were earlier in the puberty cycle than boys, and that was the problem and I'll show you mine if you will show me yours was the game some of them played with me bac k then and I guess it was an education of a sort to us all, it seemed more of a game that was played than anything else back then, but in grammar school it seemed more real and with more feelings than curiosity

I felt very emotional with some girls at that time, I think its called puppy love now but I remember some very happy relationships with girls back in the puppy love days, and given a little more time together could have grown into the real thing of that I am sure, and I like every other young kid had my favorite cute girls that I just could not make up my mind about, I liked something very much about each of them, and I know it does not go on like that forever eventually someone becomes number one, usually by graduation time every boy and girl have either found a potential mate or has made a career choice and moved into the adult world.

Guess I didn't do I right I had a different problem, I felt bad and sad that I could not compete with my peers because of my clothes we were poor and the way we came to school each year dressed proved it, I got laughed at and giggled at by some of my school mates and it made me angry, and ashamed plus that created problems with some of the boys, we very seldom got invites to parties or other teen activities I was an outcast,. it was kinda embarrassing to have all kinds of money and and can't use it.

Party time 1943

I was only invited to one party by the tenth grade, I heard about them, but was never on the list. Poverty, puberty, and pride, that was my problem in school and added up to a very angry young man who was mad at everything and everybody and had no idea how to cope with my situation so I rebelled and fought a tough hard battle with myself and others who were using me as an example to control other rebellious kids.so when I could not be controlled they got rid of me., and I had no idea how fortunate that was going to prove to be until later, it was a life changing event for the better.for me and the greatest thing that I learned from all this was, things change, today, and tomorrow will not be exactly the same, a year from today things will be different and

I will be different, Hang on and Wait!! That's What Life is all about. Until It's Over.

PUBERTY. BIG. CHANGES
Teens and HARMONES.

Every parent knows or at least has some knowledge from experience about puberty. Too bad they don't share with us teens,, we all went through it, but most of us have no idea how it occurs, or how dangerous it can be to teens, but it is a time of some large changes in our adolescent lives._Time for a new body. A vice we all have to contend with, when we reach a certain age our brain releases a hormone that starts a cycle of physical and mental changes, that hormone is called "Gonadotropin. it goes to our pituitary gland that is located under the brain, then this gland releases two more of its hormones called "luteinizing" and "Follicle" hormones,

Boys and girls both have these two hormones, however they affect them differently, with the boys they affect the testes and they start producing the hormone "testosterone" this hormone is responsible for the male body and physical appearance, and affects the sexual organs and desires and will start in most boys about the age of 9_-to 15 these same two hormones affects girls by about the age of 7___ to 13 these hormones affects sexuality. and targets the girls ovaries creating the hormone "Estrogen" and starts preparing her body for pregnancy and bearing children.

But in some instances the child's body is not prepared to receive an adult dose of these hormones, which occurs frequently., because not all boys or girls body's can be considered the same, and do not mature at the same rate, some girls that are only 13 can have a body that has matured and could pass for 18, and some boys are very muscular and have to shave at 14 others smaller even at 18_.and have little evidence of a beard the "Follicle" hormones produce the facial and pubic and body hair at a given time..that is only the physical effects that hormones have on us, the mental effects are much more definitive the brain eventually is flooded with all of these completely new hormones that cause a lot of conflict with the old way of thinking, plus there is a spurt of sudden growth in both boys and girls the physical changes are at times challenging to ourselves and to our parents.

The mental changes and sexual urges affects our lives more than anything else because what was normal yesterday is not normal today, sexuality, was not a problem before, but with all these hormones raging thru your brain and young body., Sex is now it is one of the emerging problems that causes 750,000 teenage pregnancies each year in the U S A. and only about 2% of the fathers of these baby's marry the teen mothers, what does that do for her chances of a career if she ever graduates high school, Too late for the "pill"__ This would occupy a lot of your family's thoughts and can now, create a great amount of mental and financial trouble if a pregnancy occurs in a fourteen year old daughter, its not a parent controlled thing any more, and you have no experience as how to act, or to become a mother, You must control these new urges.

And sex is a lurking demon, it is always a powerful form of persuasion for boys and girls, who can't wait to try it. The rules have changed, you now have to make some very difficult decisions that will reflect on who and what you are any how you will, be judged by your peers, and your teachers and parents., and this is a long and often difficult thing for some of us to do. This is when we need some help defining and learning to control our sexual feelings, and information from someone whom you can confide in and trust. Your parents or Usually a professional in this field.

If only there was a hormone to calm us while these mental storms are raging thru our lives as teens it could be a more pleasant experience, and now is the time most teens resort to drugs of different types to escape the helplessness that they feel with the changes in their bodies. also this is the time that they need a consultant for sexual desires. and understanding from the parents, and get professional help if necessary, and this would save us a lot of mental confusion., Abortions, and mistakes, some of them fatal. Adult hormones are a necessary event in our transitioning to adulthood. Some 60% of boys and girls make the transition with very few problems the others are not so fortunate, but it is a certainty that its coming to visit us all and a warning and some good advice would help that other forty % do a smoother transition and prevent a lot of mental and sometimes physical anguish.

Our body's at times want one thing and our brain wants something else and sex is one that don't give up easily. at puberty. "hormones" nothing but problems.Its very hard to grow up in a new body., with hormones controlling every aspect of your thoughts. welcome to your teens! good luck.you are going to need it for the next few years. or so until adulthood is reached., we do learn from our mistakes, and every one makes them, including parents and teachers.

And most of the adults in your life are still trying to forgive themselves for things they did back then, its called "Experience", so you are not alone, we are all human beings and are not perfect ourselves. but are trying to save you from yourselves., some day you will be doing the same for your child.and most of us don't want to talk about it..especially to our own children, but maybe we should! advice to a teen about sex usually only heightens their curiosity about it, but parental education about this message works more often than not..Gain their trust, Teach them about the results of failure, Those are the most dramatic. And repeat as necessary, when necessary, and as often as necessary!!and be prepared to elaborate if necessary.

A well informed teen with all the facts is less likely to succumb to passion and promiscuous sex, it will never be eliminated, but more responsible teenagers are possible..if we the parents don't shirk our responsibility to our children. Parents in my time had no ideas about the problems we have today, they were kept busy on the farm with no rest and chores to perform that required most of the strength and stamina that they possessed and were too tired at days end to think about anything but rest and sleep, plus if a girl was found to be "In a family way" she was promptly sent away to some distant relative to bear the child and it was considered shameful to her family. it was to be hidden from everyone in the community, times have changed, most boys and girls in today's world after school only have their homework and T V time to worry about.and plenty of opportunities with both parents working to "Hang out" and have sex.

If they want to and with nothing else to do, sexual activities are first choice's, then the boys brag about it in school, and now even some of the girls also talk it up about some "hot" guy they have indulged in it with., it's got to be a sport with some of them, 750,000 pregnancies per year? That seems like a lot of young lives to ruin with sex. We parents need to do something! That's a lot of grandkids, "Sex and Time" two things man can't stop, but we can control both with some effort. A twelve year old slut is not something to be proud of in any family.and hormones caused it all, and it is a joint effort caused by hormones and uninformed teens and sometimes family failure to educate the teens. about promiscuous sexual encounters before marriage. And girls a blow job is not the same as a goodnight kiss no matter what he tells you.

SMOKES 1948

You would never suspect how much trouble a pack of smokes could cause unless you were me. All I wanted that Sunday afternoon was to go to the city swimming pool in town and should have gone to the swimming hole instead, my dad gave me a dollar and then ask if I would go by a store and pick up him three packs of Camels, they were twenty cents a pack at that time, and yes kids could buy them then, that left forty cents change it cost twenty

twenty five cents to get into the pool now only fifteen Cents remain a coke was five cents now I'm down to ten cents and everything went as planned until I went into the locker room to put my clothes on_ to leave the pool ___ the fact that I had three packs of Camels was noticed by a certain seventeen year old troublemaker it seemed we had several of these in and around town, So he took them and smacked me around a little took the dime from me also I go home minus the smokes and the 10 cents and after telling my dad how this occurred he headed for town walking.

I got dressed and went to town also to church later, did not see my dad anywhere _later while in church someone approached me and said someone wants to see you outside _so I go out the church door and there is the same guy that took dads camel cigs. on the front stoop of the church, "with a pocket knife and he tried to cut my throat, I threw up my right arm and the knife cut my right arm above the wrist!! I was startled by this and turned and ran up the sidewalk to an open gas station and into the rear area where i remembered where the tire tools were kept and, grabbed up a large hammer used on truck tires and as he came in the door I threw it at his head, it hit the door frame, now it was his turn to run, I had a long tire iron and was charging him with it! with blood pouring from my arm, now I am totally pissed!! I chased him across the street into the Presbyterian Church, yard and up a tree he went, the language outside the church caused a crowd to gather, and evidently someone over at the gas station called the police because, here they are.on the scene, It was the asst. chief he called for the trouble maker to come down from the tree, but "no way "he said. Not until I was away from there with the tire iron., I'm still bleeding, someone from the church put gauze on it and taped it, took away my tire iron then I was placed into the police car, before he came down from the tree.

After interviewing everyone from all three places the officer informed me that my dad and his older brother were both in jail that my dad had encountered his brother first while looking for him and a fight had occurred, and both were jailed, Now however everything changed, the troublemaker was arrested for assault with deadly weapon and my dad released, Ruined my church nite, my dad's teeth, and no one knows where the three packs of Camel cigarettes went At least the Officer took us home in the police car, next day before my dad got smokes again.My arm healed I still wear the scar I was told by one of my brothers years later that that. The same troublemaker was killed in the Georgia State Prison. Why I don't know. Probably attitude adjustment.!That killed lots people down in the state. Prison.

Cigarettes 1948

I myself started smoking at about fourteen or so I think "Wings" was the brand because they were longer than other brands and only cost ten cents, there was no pot back in those days only rabbit tobacco and we had (no tax in those days) and smoking in the boys room!! was the thing to do to agitate the warden, and mine were long enough to "pinch" I got two. Session's with mine instead of one cheaper also money was a factor always one of. My buddy's got me started smoking in the seventh grade I think, I didn't particularly like it but it was "the thing to do, did made me dizzy a few times also everyone else was doing it so I joined them. Wished a thousand times I had not.

Bad habit

Now Bumming a smoke sometimes created a problem depends how it was done, if you ask nicely, normally guys would take out the pack and shake one loose for you, proper etiquette was "thanks" most of us boys wore tee shirts with a pocket, after the shirt was worn a few times the pocket sagged a little but when someone walked up to you flicked your smokes out of your shirt pocket caught them on the fly took one and stuck the pack into his pocket, oops. Wrong approach, that's not bumming that's stealing. Usually it depended entirely on who it was and how good a friend he was as to the outcome of that maneuver,.Happened to me one night, one of my buddy's older brother, he would not give them back to me, he he was he was about twenty one or so and told me I was too little to be smoking. And a few other things I won't repeat, or go into He was most likely correct. About the smoking part, anyway But the fact remained he just stole my smokes, and some of the other words were a reflection on my mothers good name so_I lined him up stepped off the curb hit him just under the left eye just as hard as I could don't know what form of insanity i possessed that night but, He lucked out no cars were coming he was out, laying on the white line middle of the street.I walked out got my smokes put them back in my pocket as all my buddy's watched i then turned and went into the drugstore and sat down. whew!!! O man!!! I can't believe that I just did that to that guy, Damn, he was twice my size it just made me furious and without thinking about the consequences i had just reacted, first impulse was what I did, and I should have let it go. but that would have sent the wrong message to those there watching.all I could think was get out of here quick as you can, but no one knew it but my insides were shaking like a leaf in a hurricane, someone poured a glass of water in his face and got him up and out of the street and he went home..

Then and only Then did my breathing go back to normal, I stayed out of his way for a long _ long time after that. This guy was twenty five I found out and twice my size and weight, All that over a ten cent pack of smokes, Next time I saw him he half way apologized and ask if I was mad at him?

I said no problem on my part,_ and we were cool again. He ask after that, when bumming a smoke from anyone around town, and I was nervous around him for a very long time. But nothing was ever said that would indicate that he was going to get even with me for it, so I got back to normal around him.None of my friends ever attempted to do that they always ask when bumming a smoke, and so did I, they were expensive ten cents a pack.ten cents would get you a banana split at the drug store fountain then. with three dips of ice cream, and a cherry on top!!.a lot healthier, and a lot less dangerous.but i was a feisty little dude in those days. how I stayed alive I will never know, but most of my crowd of friends had manners, please, and thanks worked better than a fist.

Pool shark1950

Pool rooms were a good place to lose every dime you got. One of my my buddy's was a master at the game of pool.He was only about five ft three an walked kinda funny and wore clod hopper shoes, chewed Beech Nut tobacco, drank beer, He would set up a sucker by shooting the worst game that anyone could imagine, and I would win a five buck game a a few _ times in a row, then I would just barely let him win the game and someone else would challenge him for the table he would just manage to win, and the $ would escalate up as far as the challenger wanted to go and after some sloppy shooting and seemingly lucky shots he would win again. Just luck he said to to the opponent, This continued until the loser gets smart and realizes he has been "Hustled" by a pro and quits, but there is always another one who thinks he can beat him and a lot of one hundred dollars games are played, the first of these was my clue to make like a tree and "leave" we roomed together down the street about four blocks on Cain street in Atlanta,

He had a few thousand dollar nights at the "Q "room down by the Bus Station without getting his ass beat._now I was a fair shooter but avoided the big games fifty cents was my limit, he managed a pool room up in North Atlanta for eight years and could beat me shooting a game with one hand behind his back his favorite trick, was to act drunk with a hundred dollars in his pocket usually shirt pocket so it could be seen by all present, and it worked about 99% of the time, then, I would challenge him and beat him for ten or twenty dollars three or four times and a. New

challenger called me and I would loose to him. Then Then my buddy would challenge him.
And loose a few

Ten dollar games to get the game price up to big $$ then he would borrow five hundred of his money from me, that i carried for him and I would leave, then he went to work and would run the table on you, And some of them wanted to try it again double or nothing!! With him that exactly what he wanted you to do lucky if you had your shirt and shoes when you finally quit He was not just good, He was a professional hustler.sloppy dresser, talked really country fied like a hayseed from the sticks.

And he never lost a game of pool unless he wanted to. Sometimes he got roughed up a bit by sore losers but, he expected it and remained passive and refused to fight, Management at the place usually broke up the rowdy boys and threw them out, or called the cops.& old buddy boy laughed all the way home. He later got drafted into the army I was told and after a year or so was diagnosed with Diabetes and received a medical Discharge, went back to his old ways, drank too much and Died in his forties in the mid seventies my buddy in the fifyiess.He.lived a rough life, guess he had little or no education so he used what he had the talent for.and believe me he never missed, my old pal, a areal pool shark. And my good and loyal friend, Cowboy.

RACEING 1950----1988

If my dad had any idea what went on out in my world back then he most likely would have Never handed me the keys to that light green Ford pickup truck when I had enough money in the "Bank of Prince Albert" to buy my own truck, some of the older "Misfits" in town. that owned their own cars would like to have a little Road Race ten dollar entry fee. Saturday night about midnight from the town of Canton Ga.to a drive Drive In Restaurant in North Atlanta a total of about forty five miles

Winner Take All was the only rule Winner also has to buy the beer..Now that means we have to draw a pill (bingo numbers) from a box for starting position low numbers line up side by side front to rear and you run what you bring now my dads p/up truck was not in the class of some of these boys cars.

But I loved the race the first ten miles were open road then you hit my home town and twenty five crazy car drivers at times close to a hundred thru town was not sport to the police, so they stayed out of the way ___ eight miles further was Sandy Springs.

Same thing with cops there, very seldom see any of them unless a wreck occurred then on to North Atlanta before one am For Last Call For Alcohol Was made.,.I never won but had lots of fun, Lots of Excitement, so was dirt track racing most all of the first NASCAR'S drivers were at one time "Trippers" moonshine that's how they learned to drive so good so fast. It was a deadly game we played with the cops. If my dad had any idea. I would be Grounded for life would have been a real possibility.. A race car of my own was always my dream, and finally with a little help from my cousin Don. He being a little older than I got our hands on a little. Ford coupe put in the roll bars did a few other minor things like removing the glass and lights, mirrors, etc. got it ready to run Towed it to Atlanta to the Peach Bowl race track a quarter mile oval dirt track, lots of talent got their start at these little tracks.

Over in the stinky stock yards and he drove it one heat race and that was enough for him never again he said, too much speed not enough control, that's when I got my real start at being a serious racer I loved it. Saturday night dirt track racing, gets into your blood, Still does I raced for ten years, finally had to quit family got too big for to race. Wife and 3 kids 25 years old. I raced Go Karts for for a year or more after giving up the dirt track cars, bought my first airplane several years later. But, That's another story.Danger and I were good friends at the time. I still can't go to a dirt track race today, I want to go home and start building a race car. I still feel the need for speed it's the competition that's really the problem I know. I loved the competition I built both my older son's race cars, and one for my wife Taught them to become competitive at the track, and in life.you gotta learn to win some and lose some because that's what we all do in real life to learn how to contend with losing, and get better next time keep trying and eventually it will happen.

I always wanted to drive Daytona back when they ran on the beach, I loved that race.I lost more than my share of races because of poor or cheap equipment, as I was learning, took 5 years to win a race, I really didn't have the money to be competitive with guys who had big dollar sponsors but I had to try, I was more the go kart budget type, and it satisfied my need for speed.and I won a lot.and that satisfied my ego. _and we all need to win sometimes, it feels so good! When you do. And its an excellent motivation technique to do your best at everything you do_ The path to success is very elusive.to people who give up easily.

HORNET HUNTING 1949

Of course we young sprouts loved to go hunting after school if we didn't have orders from headquarters(mom or dad). My two hunting buddies were both experienced hunters and one had a beautiful pair of Red Setter Bird dogs that loved a hunt I was not allowed to have a shotgun but got a huge knife and scabbard for christmas at seven years old. Mom. Was real happy about that and took it away after removing it from the top of my foot where my brother had thrown it, we were just practicing our Daniel, l Boone knife throwing skills.dont know what mom. Did with them afraid to ask.

So I had to borrow this twelve gauge from a neighbor, it was a sawed off double barrel twelve guage that packed a powerful kick when fired so I seldom fired unless I was sure of a hit. Once over in a swamp (pasture) there was a giant Hornets nest hanging from a limb of a tree that grew in size as the weeks went by until it was Huge this one was the largest one I had ever seen and there were lots of them.

That's when I decided to blow it apart with the double barrel shotgun I don't remember if my hunting buddies were with me or not But I walked right up to it and fired both barrels into it and of thousands Hornets in there I must have killed at least three and the fact that I had just destroyed their home really pissed them off. Now if you have never Been stung by an extremely pissed off hornet you have missed an important event, in your life, that you will cherish for life, if you live over it.

You have never experienced the most excruciating pain conceivable to the human body until. Then, I don't have any idea how many were after me. But I do know how many got me, I dropped the 12 gauge And ran as fast as I ever had, until the first one stung me and then I established my all time 100 yard dash record in to the near by Creek, it was only about knee deep____ not deep enough for me I almost drowned fighting and splashing around the hornets did not seemed to be impressed by all these antics and continued to Sting me at will, I finally ran down the creek and got away.

I had taken twenty five direct hits and before I could get home I became violently ill and started vomiting, I finally got home and mom bathed my back with cold compresses until I calmed down, my brother went over and got the gun after dark, that was another close call for me in my dumber years.dont ever mess with Hornets. They are not friendly! Much worse than high school principals!!, But boys have to learn. And usually the hard way, but these hornets do leave a lasting impression!.it hurts now just thinking about them., and that was about sixty five years ago in.forty nine, my hunting buddies back then. In the Good ole Days!!.another painful lesson learned the hard way. The nerve of those hornets stinging me like that, about a week later I wrapped an old rag around my longest cane fishing pole and saturated it with gasoline went back over to the hornets home and burned it down with, a lot of vengeance in my heart.I don't get mad I get even! _(That's southern pride talking) ____Mr..Hornet!!

THE CRANE 1951

The summer I came back to Ga. From Alabama to live with my aunt and uncle he told me one bright sunshine morning as we were having our breakfast together that he would like It., if I would go with him to his job site and help him with something, I wasn't sure what he did, but on the way there he explained he was a P&H crane operator and it was time for the cables and clutches to be checked on his machine.for safety.reasons on the job, So when we arrived, I helped pull out all of the steel cable on the crane, this was a huge machine He looked at every inch of the cable first then went inside the machine and showed me how it operated started it up and rewound the cable explained to me how the brakes on the cables worked how it turned and how it crawled, He was very good with this thing I decided before that day was over. we "oiled" it as he called it and did all the maintenance that was due to be done to it. then explained why he preferred to do this himself rather than the company maintenance man, he kept records himself on this machine that he referred. to as "His" machine.

He was familiar with every inch of this thing how it felt how it moved how it reacted to his touch. About a week later he ask how would I like a part time job with him in the summer, wow!!! What could I do? They were building concrete walls along the new freeway of. interstate seventy five thru the Peachtree and Spring street section of Atlanta that year so I was shown how to ride the concrete bucket on my uncles machine and taught the hand signals to him to put me over the concrete pour areas to the forms it was an exciting job.at times and some fancy foot work up there sometimes, high up in the air on some of those walls with the boom way up on the crane, and it was a little scary, I was there at times when needed that summer, and good pay!!! We poured a Lot of Concrete, and I gave some money to my aunt and bought nice clothes for my Senior fall school year it was a great feeling to be able to do this for myself. And for the first time I had a legal bank account with help from my aunt

PAT 1951

And if it was OK with my aunt and with my girlfriends mother and father he was pastor of the church, I went over on Wed. and Sat. Nights to go to church with her, her dad stayed after services most nights so she and I walked back to the little park just past her house for our, hugging and kissing we could see her house from the park so when mom and dad came home so did we, gotta stay in good with them. I don't think they were as carefree about her as I thought. She was an only child and I often wondered if they knew anything about me.they never ask me much about anything outside of school and my grades. My situation at the time was kept quiet by everyone..... I was being a very good boy, and enjoying it very much.

Good things were coming to me now and it was the happiest I had ever been in my life.But in the back of my mind I was scared to death...That it was too good to be this elated..helplessness plagued me constantly....ok puberty What's next? and while writing this I learned of her possible Death in twenty eleven_if so _she will make a wonderful addition to God's Heaven And I can't blame him for wanting you back there with him,. And I still think about the big overall picture of how some things work out sometimes in our lives, our wants needs and dreams don't always work out and what If some things in life you never forget. And some things you leave behind, And she still occupies an area in my past that is extremely important to me even today a beautiful example of what all girls could and should be. God sure knew what he was doing when he made her. And gave you to your parents, and I still think at times, what if I had the fortitude to have told you and your parents about my less than squeaky clean past, what's the worst thing that could have happened? Would it have been any worse?

Guess it was not meant to be. It's my only excuse now, but was it puberty in action, to blame for the whole mess I made of my early life? or a combination of things and events as I suspect? Or did i just want to grow up too fast and break too many rules doing it? Trying to eradicate most of my personal problems?did I go too far too fast,?after all I was still just a kid, but some of my escapades were dangerous, and I was blind to all that,__Just plain dumb luck? I still don't really know even today, what truly motivated me to do some of those things, but I got away with it clean and free.I blame it on poverty, and my puberty.and hard headed pride. After you read this, my story, you decide!!! The cause Not the effect.!

HUNTING AND FISHING 1939

Back in forty six_we kids were armed and dangerous We had slingshots and a pocket full of rocks it don't get any more dangerous than that, nothing was safe from that we could actually hit things we aimed at after a summer or two of practice, birds would rather fly "over the cuckoo's nest" than close to us. we actually went squirrel hunting with these things, and with marbles instead of rocks got a few for the pot at home, and if you wanted to get on my dad's good side, bring in a couple of squirrels for mom to make squirrel and dumplings with for him, Everyone else preferred them fried nice and brown and milk gravy and hot biscuits.

My brother and I referred to them as "Tree Rats" but not in dads presence or at the eating table, good way to get smacked hard. We ate lots of different foods mom was an excellent cook and nothing went to waste, leftovers were in day after tomorrow's soup and even that was delicious, mom always said anything was good if you were hungry. And at times we were. Absolutely famished, after a full day of school and a afternoon of working over at the sawdust pile in the woods cutting stove wood for the trip to Atlanta next Saturday morning. And thinking back a few years.

Some nights back in the thirtys food was kinda short mom would not send us to bed hungry, we had milk and we had corn meal she would boil corn meal with onions and put that in a glass and cover it with milkThat's called cornmeal mush and onions and it was good!!.filled our little belly's up. Worry about tomorrow, Tomorrow.

The Good Lord Will Provide. mom said, and between the two of them somehow we made it. Mom was the one that told me how to make a rabbit box(trap) and between the 2 of us we did. And it worked. And we caught quite a few in the fall and winter, we never ate rabbits in the summer. Her rule. Upon occasion we had to kill a chicken, but she decided which one, I later learned that some of them quit laying eggs and started appearing on our kitchen table for that offence, some of them were old and tough, but mom said that "they made the gravy stink" And we ate them and the gravy. We had cane fishing poles and sometimes, in the afternoon after the crops were laid by (That means that we have done all that needs to be done to them) she would jump up from her chair grab me give me a big hug and say..

"Let's go fishing"!!! Get your pole!!! And hurry up the fish are bitting I can hear them from here!!! She And i gathered up my little brother in his basket and down thru the pasture to the creek we would go, then down the creek to a large lake(sometimes we had to dig worms first) or catch dragon flies for bait, small grasshoppers worked well also.two or three of those large mouth bass made my day, The lake belonged to our neighbors down the road about a half mile or so, mom usually knew where a caterpillar worm nest was, and they were good bait, and we would catch a mess of fish for supper!!!.talk about Good!!!Yum.!! Gravy and hot biscuits too, My mom was a very Smart lady.!! in 1939. BC. (before chickens)

FOR THE GOOD TIMES 1947

Today it is impossible to even imagine some of the conditions that some of my relatives in the past had to endure, I have read extensively in books about poverty and its effects on human behavior and the quest that led some people to different forms of behavior, but back in my childhood with two slightly different Religions between my parents, the trust in God was the only hope they had, then And faith that existed in the people in those days was phenomenal and compared to today when we have what those people were praying for back then, and didn't have any idea if or when it would come.

To pass or not and now that we have our good fortune, It took a lot of different people and a lot of different prayer, my girl friend as i liked to call her back then, they were another good influence on me i would have done anything for her, those girls and some others that helped Me to be alive today, they gave me a lot of good advice and talked me out of many of my stupid ideas at the time or else there would have much more to this story, and they gave me some "Anger management" talks because they didn't want me to get in trouble, Most of them have now married and moved on, but I have not forgotten them or what they helped me with, they were some of my favorite people then.

The Fab Four i called them It was tough growing up the way I had to but, I had no other choice, I was the product of my environment, now I can see that it helped to make a much better person of me later in my life, compassion is a bitter pill sometimes lots of things could have gone wrong for me back then and enough did, could have been much worse if I had been found out about some things, I was pretty slick for my age, "Idle hands are the Devils tools" my mom used to say so she kept mine busy Picking Cotton & feeding Chickens.for years.Fart

And cleaning out the mess the chickens left us, I had just enough freedom to grow up as a boy in the circumstances that prevailed at that time in my life. I was a good worker and always finished whatever chore she gave me and did it to the best of my ability, and she liked and appreciated that. I got lots of "atta_boys, from my mom for the help, And a lot of the old _"Sayings" she used have came to mind at the appropriate time that little voice back in my head sometimes changed my course of action that I was about to take, She and many of my school mates had a much more influencing role in me than I realized until I was older. Thanks mom!!!

THE THE FAB 4 1947--1949

GIRLS ECT.

Thanks you were a great bunch! Of girls why I used to wonder are boys so stupid and girls so smart?____none of you Fab Four know it., But many times in my later professional life I gave a lot of ladies a chance at a job that normally was a man thing to perform, and any other man would not have considered, a woman doing it. I created lots of first with the ladies in my career and they became Great!!!and I got ostracized by many other men for doing it. And I got my share of phone calls from other men in my position at other facilities with the question of,_ "Do you realize what you have started? Yes ____ yes I do was my response.great isn't it?

I just gave another lady a chance to do something another way than a man would have done it, another opportunity to expand her knowledge and skill and mine, so I'm really going to be one of the winners in this endeavor I'm not as stupid as I look I use to tell the guys.don't underestimate the girls, they will fool you every time!!!I was proud of the way some of them went on to bigger and better things even tho they had to leave me to accomplish it.All they were waiting for was an opportunity to come their way get that all important "Track Record" they had the talent that was needed. To do the job, And I recommended them highly.and I was sincere about it. And we remained friends and shared information with each other over many subjects, for many years. The women in my life, personally and professionally, have shown and shared more information and good sense with me than the men, if you are successful in your endeavors men are either resentful, or jealous not so with the girls. I was never afraid that someone else could take my job, I was always positive in my attitude and insisted on honesty and professional courtesy in our relations with our customers, and if you can get my job by being better than me, Go for it you are welcome to it, Never had it happen though.I always kept the confidentiality rules that applied with my superiors, and demanded professional results from my personell.cheat, steal, or lie, we parted company.That was a certainty.I was friends with them all, and respected their knowledge and ability,

If-- they desired to be schooled better in their specialty, they got it!, I wanted the best, and I enjoyed helping them to become the best.that gets you respected, makes for better paydays, happier wives, and families, which in turn makes your attitude better____ and round and round it goes!!!., "happy people do better work". The attitude of working with me not against me made me a better manager and improved my reputation also.

GETTING REAL 1950--1951

The 3 Rs. Reading__Riteing __& Rithmetic Were the fundamentals that we all had to learn in school, but I favored History, Geography, and spelling, Arithmetic would have been much easier if I had had a Real. Teacher rather than what I had, the two of us had a personality conflict She could not teach me anything, and unfortunately I could not learn anything from her. Kinda like trying to nail Jello to a tree, Today, I think it was her Domineering attitude that offended me the most my mom always said I was like a length of chain, You could lead or love me into doing anything, but don't try pushing me, I just wadded up on you and she was mostly correct., I was at the time the chairman of the ways and means committee, I had more ways of being mean than anyone you ever met and I absolutely hated to be forced to do anything. Still Do!!.And don't strike me I take that very personal (my dad did not abide by this rule at all) And I. always Retaliate and I promise it will embarrass you or hurt you in some way just as my dad learned one night, now this also, Included women, Please.

_Never put yourself in a mans place by hitting or cursing a man if you are a woman moms rule__if you are a lady, act like one, not a man!. And for heaven's sake save it, wait till he calms down before telling him how to go to hell, and making him look forward to the trip. that's called finesse.

A real woman has other *ways" of making us sorry for whatever the confrontation might have been about, I learned that one the hard way also. My last whipping I took from dad was from a piece of garden hose about thirty inches long that was for not having the chickens fed before he got home from work at seven pm. I was black and blue all over from that one. mom was also "very" upset about that, and I'm sure he heard about it And the next night at the supper table, I told him that it was the last one!!! Don't ever try it again, I won't take it!! First time I ever had the balls to talk back to him, I was surprised at his reply OK. He said. looking up at me, The next time was the night up in the country when I had been brought home about 2 am inebriated and we Had one hell of a fight. That was the last one mom said Allen!!. "Don't ever do that. again or I will Brain you with an iron frying pan" she told my dad, and he never did, We finally became almost friends About time, I was sixteen going on seventeen years old.and I had almost forgot what it was like back home, my dad and his brother were two totally completely different people.my uncle was more successful than my dad, but they only had one child not seven and were financially secure, nicer home and fewer worries, much different attitude with his son and me.a totally different world for me, no stress. "peaceful" a new and completely environment, i loved it.!! But at times I was still homesick,

Foster home 1945

My early school experience at the elementary grades were pleasant enough although the teacher was the "Boss" and I had a run in the first day of the 6 th grade with my new teacher, now I was known to tease just in fun at times, but on the first day, each of us had to stand and tell our name our mom and dad's name how many brothers and sisters we ha I guess that had some,

Significant amount of importance to the teacher, or it was a test of your self confidence who knows__anyway when it came my turn I explained that I was a Foster child and lived in a Foster home, my name and that I had 1 Foster sister and 3 Foster brothers, being the compassionate soul that she was, she came to my desk hugged me tightly, kissed my cheek and said" O Bless Your Heart "darling", and gave me that warm and fuzzy feeling, all over.

How ever that compassion had been dramatically dissipated by the next day, when I appeared at class _She had learned that I had put one over on her and she was not one to be trifled with_She grabbed me by the shirt collar, drug me out into the hallway and proceeded to set my little butt on fire with a switch, and chided me for making a fool of her the day before,!!! And left me standing in the hall until the lord's prayer and pledge of allegiance to the flag was done, only then was I invited back into the room to class with the warning more was to come if I was naughty any more._ and I never tried to sell her any of my smart pills either, now this lady was about six ft tall and two hundred twenty pounds not a woman to trifle with, she was a wonderful teacher and I grew to love that lady.(she never had to take me out in the hallway again) and I think she said she had never had children of her own, but she loved us all. And sometimes did catch us love bugs passing notes to each other in class but never embarrassed us by making us stand and read them aloud to the class, unlike other teachers, while everyone giggled!!! She understood young love.and did not stand in it's way.. A wonderful lady!!! She is also the teacher that told me that my cuticle was showing, and I told her that I had told my mom that these pants were too short, she kept me after class and explained it to me. And I never forgot.

Battle of of love 1946

After my loosening the battle of love with a certain girl I was depressed for a month or so nothing was right anymore, I tried dating her sister a few times but she was bonkers for another boy from over across the river, so I gave up on her. I had enough problems already, and I was still getting in more trouble at school than I could handle, thinking back, I think I just didn't care what became of me, I kinda stumbled along not giving a damn about anything, for a period of time, kinda like a bad dream, Lovesickness is really what it was i guess, That was a new sensation for me, I was always a kinda carefree guy so I sat down with a small bottle of Jack Daniels one Saturday afternoon about dark up at the Baptist Church and had a talk with my dead Grandmother.

For a few hours And she assured me that as I got older things would improve and not to give up that as long as there was life there was hope, things will change. Cheer up things could be worse__ so I cheered up, and sure enough things got worse!, Much worse, like a housefly under a cow pile, I had to dig my way out, because I felt the whole world was against me, Depression I think they call it today, and it was Much much later things got better, it seems like another world opened up for me just getting out of the local school system and my home life was an immediate improvement, I didn't realize what another environment could do for your attitude on life, there really was another way to live, and I loved it. But I still had a lot of doubts and fears because some day this was going to end, then what do I do.? Then? Another wait and see!!!.another decision!!!! Life was good out with my aunt and uncle and school at a new school And a new group of friends and a new girl that interested me greatly and I for the first time in my life I didn't want things..to change. I would worry about it later.

SPORTS 1950

My new environment at my new home and new school along with the time I was spending with sports and my new friends was so rewarding that my life became more like something out of a Walt Disney movie, just too perfect to be true, my grades in school were also good, I had won a hundred yard dash event in track and had helped in the eight eighty relay win at the same meet, I had a new and wonderful feeling,, "Happiness" slowly came into my life, and truthfully I didn't quite know how to react, I now loved doing things that I used to hate doing, like studying, I always hated that, and helping my aunt, by asking if there was anything I could do to help her around the house, I mowed the grass trimmed the trees, pulled the weeds, swept the sidewalk, and driveway, it was great to feel this elated now!!!

Not a worry in the world, that's the summer I got the job driving the ice cream truck and learned to play tennis in the park up in Atlanta my aunt and Uncle were not extremely happy with that situation but knew that my time with them was getting short and I needed to make some of my own decisions about my future.I was still a little insecure about something's about girls and how I felt around them im sure it showed, but I needed to gain my self confidence because most of them could out think me on most topics, but I was really good at kissing. Pattrica said, I liked that... All I was good at was fighting and acting weird, and raising hell, up to now, quite a transition for me to make in a short period of time, But girls were so complex I thought, not at all like boys, inside and out, I still sometimes don't know if I said or did the right thing when i interacted with the girls, on some things, without sounding chauvinistic I try not to but, I'm still a man!. and my belief is that women have done more for me than I ever did for them, so I have a lot of confidence in all the ladies, most of them are a heck of a lot smarter than we are and, if given the chance can really surprise people, I promise you I have learned a lot from the girls they figured it out long, long, ago, Compromise is a lot smarter than a bloody nose and a black eye, maybe there's something to this compromise thing, I thought.although doing it was uncomfortable at first I slowly realized that you don't have to win every discussion or disagreement and to be fair at times its OK to lose even when you were right. wow one of my first adult decisions.

The biggest problem seemed to be keeping my mouth shut. And waiting to be ask, if my opinion was wanted.or desired_new world!!!.sweet. learning fineness was another attribute, that required some practice in the real world, its not easy to tell someone to go to hell __and make them look forward to the trip. _Now that is fineness in action.!!!

A lot of lessons to be learned yet young squirt. My mom used to tell me yes indeed mom_ yes indeed!!!.And it was still true even then!.and I was learning some of the correct things to say and do for my first time and it amazed me sometimes that I was really able to do this and enjoy it, No muss no fuss no bother, what a difference a few months and a new environment had done to me.. And I liked it..and I felt good inside..this was all new to me, I had not had a fist fight about anything in a long time strange!!!

Maybe there was hope for me yet, no insults, no name calling, no proving who was the biggest or the baddest, no bullying, a new world!!! Now how to cope and adjust without looking hayseed stupid. This is what you have been wanting is it not?

More news 1950

The world keeps turning, and the changes keep on coming, some good and some not so good and at fourteen years old some decisions made in haste and anger don't work out for your best interest or your future, and at fourteen my future was tomorrow and my interest was subject of a lot of circumstances, basically it wasn't a sure thing at all on anything or anybody I was not worried about my future, my concern was today and tomorrow can worry about itself.

I lived one hour at a time, and at times 1 minute at a time, I never knew what was next, it was a crazy way to live, then I had to go home, that was another time zone in itself, I never knew what mood dad was going to be in, another uncertainty to deal with, seems like I spent most of that period of my life dealing with uncertainties about everything and after a period of time this leads to hostilities. that are hard to control along with the puberty factors that I have to contend with also fifteen is or can be a terrifying time with emotions running rampant thru your mind, and sadly some of us go too far and over the edge, far too many teens lose it completely and commit suicide _and at times I walked around mad at the world and because no one notices that we are in serious emotional trouble, mostly from hormones and their effects on certain types of the teens.and no one i don't think at that age you really wish to become an Axe murder.

Why this is not taught in health classes in mid and high school freshman years I have no idea, I only know that it would have been of tremendous value to me personally, to help understand the rapid emotional and mental storms that rage thru some of us at that period in our lives Emotionally, love and hate are not far apart in the human species, and a good school class could explain a lot to this age group, I'm not talking about sex education classes call them Social transition classes, or puberty101 male class and the same for girls, give us some information about what is happening to us, and what to expect in our puberty stage, but it Was not to be,

In my case I had to be in the Juvenile justice system for that explanation by a "Shrink" and I was not the only one there for the same aggressive, or depressive reasons, we were let down by our Educational system in our Public Schools.and in most instances our parents don't know how to tell teens things we need to know._ Boys are not the only ones that need this program there were just as many girls in the program at Juvi. As boys. About 95% of our parents are not aware or ignore this, not all of the teens need it, but those that do are important to society as a person.and deserve some help at or before it happens to them. Emotional confusion is a very hard thing to fight alone, especially now that the flood of hormones are added to this equation.

And if you have no idea what the problem is, how do you deal with it?you can do some of the most stupid things at this time, and regret it later and at times i wondered why i had said or did some things? and now with the inter net and computers!the gay guys prey on a lot of our children without out the parents even suspecting that anything is amiss, until its all over the net and the child is humiliated to the point of self destruction, All teens are subjected to some rapid changes in our body's And our Emotions,, and we will not cry for help, but we still need it._parents need to watch and monitor any rapid changes in behavior girls more so than boys, puppy love or a smooth talking young adult can destroy their life I on the other hand had to learn everything the hard way, and so did everyone else, that's why we had a swimming hole on the creek, and boys and girls both got that part of their sex education there, the natural way. And we never had a problem it was self policed with our own values. Plus there was safety in numbers We were Different physically and Emotionally but we were the same otherwise.

We were kids trying to become adults.some the easy way and some the hard way., I was in the latter!!!.I never ask for any help, wasn't aware that I needed any.!! Never crossed my mind. Wish it had, could have saved me a lot of turmoil and years of anguish in my teens.I'm sorry but i had no idea that it was a natural thing, and just to relax, not to worry or become paranoid about it, no one can imagine what went thru my mind some days, some of the thoughts were terrifying and uncontrollable and all because I was not aware of what and why this happens during puberty.

The agony of ignorance is what teen suicide is all about.I can't even imagine what a gay boy or girl or a transgender teen has to endure mentally, physically or genetically at this period of their life, peer pressure alone could push them over the edge..I don't know what the complete answer is or how to advise teens on this subject, but I know that assurances by your parents and in some cases professional consultation can be very beneficial to alleviate some of the traumatic effects of the puberty stage of your life, and some adolescents just cruise thru it like it never happened, the rest of us sure make an ordeal of it, however.it is going to happen to everyone so being prepared for it and its consequences is good thing to know..

Whatever you do Don't fall into the trap of teen sex and drugs you will be tempted and coerced by your friends and peers to join in with them in this degrading activity, think!!! What will a baby now do to your future? Most likely it will end any hopes of professional success that you had planned before marriage and create a home and family crises to be dealt with immediately, and drugs are a killer of dreams they will erode your spirit and consume your pride. Don't ever go there!!! You deserve much better. Its a deep dark pit to fall into, and it won't let your mind or body rest, it keeps calling you to come deeper into pain and despair you are the only one that can save you. Just say No!!., and save your future to share with someone you love and build a life with parents its too late when your daughters are pregnant or your sons are in jail to correct the real problem!! 40% of girls loose their virginity by, age 13 another 20% by 14 another 20% by16__ only 20% make it to 18 _puberty is constantly a hormone nightmare to all teens!these stats were results from a study reported on the inter net. Done in 2014.results were a national study. Not a regional study.

Ford plant 1951

Field trips my junior year were one of the things that got my attention it was amazing to see how an automobile was assembled, a field trip down to Hapeville GA. to the Ford plant was my most memorable event in high school, watching cars come down the line lineage seeing the finished product emerge was almost unbelievable, that was my highlight of the day, and I also liked "Shop "at school it covered lots of woodworking, something that I was somewhat familiar with after helping build some houses back a few years ago, also I was the only one that had any experience with building things and my teacher kinda!et me tell and teach some of the guys about what I knew, also, I had worked with my uncle the past summer building the interstate freeways in Atlanta and rode the mud bucket pouring concrete even my teacher was impressed by that, and I'm sure the thought occurred to him that it was a case of wishful thinking, he looked at at me kinda smiled, and Ask me to come up by him and tell him and the class about such an exciting experience, and that gave me a. new feeling inside, then when I told them about driving my own race car at 15 and riding the mud bucket with my uncle the boys were really impressed, all though I don't think all of them really believed that really happened, but they didn't dispute me on it and gave me the benefit of doubt on it, but when I brought in the two trophies that I had won in competition, that did it and some pictures of the crane and me on the bucket with my hard hat on

, I had gained a lot of respect, another new feeling to me, I had never felt pride in any of the things i had done, and failed to realize that these boys lived in the city and had what i would consider a very boring life for sure they were all nice to me and I was accepted into the brotherhood of the Wildcats.

I was an accomplished young man, and didn't realize it. Wow!! And all this time I thought I was just a useless little brat, these guys were almost like fans! The first Rainbow in my life!!!! I didn't quite know how to act, Some of these guys were studs on the football field, and I finally made the team and I lettered in it and in Track my first year there_I Was so proud of myself, I didn't screw up not one time, and with that letter sweater there were GIRLS pleading to wear my sweater __ another first __ I had become somebody! What an ego trip that was.

And my girlfriend wore my sweater proudly and I was on cloud nine and for the first time in my life felt like I had accomplished something, _another new feeling that dark cloud that always followed me around seemed sad that I was happy for a change, and I was always afraid it would reappear at some inopportune moment. But at the moment it was on vacation. Most likely it would be back,__ and it was a new sensation to be free and happy and lucky to have such a great girlfriend and she was was my girl __ life was great for this Country Boy!. Was puberty done with wrecking my life,? The pride I felt was from my own accomplishments and not from having to defending myself with my fist,, and I had my own bank account and a few hundred dollars in it, why can't I shake off this feeling of dread? Am I not allowed to experience happiness? I do and I don't! Tomorrow will be another day try try again...how long can this last? Uncertainties were my constant companion.and I needed something to be sure of. Thus far trust was a big thing missing in my past, and I liked this new life and I liked the good feeling it gave me, a new experience.and I wanted it to last.for ever.But into each life some rain must fall and I knew that there was more rain in my future. Was I ready for it?

The hard way 1951

There were times after I got into my late teens, was married and had a baby of our own that I would talk to my wife about her upbringing, and found hers was so very different from mine, she was a lot meeker as a child than I was, she had very few arguments with her parents, did as she was told without any resentment just kinda did the easy way out and avoided trouble her family was just as poor as mine was she just didn't have the same fire and spirit that I did as an adolescent_ and I reflected long and hard as to why my childhood was so very difficult, and why I was not happy with the status quo, I wanted things my way, the easy way. "But that's not the way it's done" i was reminded over and over again, but I usually did it my way anyway and paid the consequences for it later and there were many of them.

STICKS AND STONES 1941

Thanksgiving of forty-six one we had a lot of relatives for dinner at our home, moms sisters and brothers came ____ The men all decided to go hunting in the late morning about 10am so guns were brought out and loaded, there were about ten or so of them naturally I wanted to go along as I had never been "Hunting" but and dad refused to let any of the youngsters go along, so we all cried and wailed for a while after they left us, later as you know "little pitchers have big ears" I heard my mom and one of her sisters talking, that the men were just off having a few "Snorts" in southern language that translates to drinking ole liker_ we were disappointed that we could not go __ so one of my cousin's suggested we go on our own, now that seemed like a good idea, so I went into the house and told mom about our idea, she said Ok but not to go over across the creek where the men were hunting __ OK..

We are good to go now so we arm ourselves with broom and broken hoe handles a few sling shots and off we go_five of us as I recall seven to twelve year olds_ so over to the broom sage patch where the rabbits "bed" we go thru and knocked three rabbits in the head, and down by the spring where the squirrels come for water we got two of them with the slingshots the older boys had so we are back home by with our kill by 1:30 pm. so these were skinned out and cooked for lunch along with the Turkey the ladies had made

The men folks came home about four pm _empty handed a little woozy with no game killed but did kill a couple of bottles and a few corn stalks they said,,, so for Thanksgiving meal they were served the game us boys got and served by a big laughing crowd of ladies and kids that had a successful hunt with sticks and slingshots than the "great white hunters" had with all those big shotguns.

Those guys heard about that for years!!!.It was not often that the ladies got the advantage on the men but that was really a good one and they teased them about maybe they should stay home and let the boys do the hunting from now on with better results.

MEAN OLE HEN 1938

Hens lay their eggs in strange places when they start "Setting" they usually lay about twelve __ eggs in a hidden nest and sit on the eggs constantly, except to eat and drink until the eggs hatch__ now these ladies usually warn you that they setting, they carry their wings down low off their back just dragging the ground and are very aggressive and will attack if molested my mom had followed a hen that had just started to set down to the barn and watched her go under it and knew that a nest full of eggs was under there __ now my job is to allow a rope to be tied to my feet and to push a pan in front of me and crawl under the barn and retrieve these eggs and at the age of 4 in I went the problem was that my mom was mistaken about the hen not being on the nest.

She definitely was!! And I was in between the floor joist of the barn floor in about an eighteen inch wide area and about the same height with Nowhere to run!!! Chicken is in my face flogging me with her wings and pecking my face, And I'm screaming and bumping my head on the barn floor and kicking my feet _ it seemed an eternity before. Mom pulled me out away from that insane chicken. After that I would not go under the barn after eggs they could Rot for all I cared.!! Mom thought it was funny and told the story on me, to everyone else in the community that wanted a good laugh at my expense, and laughed at me for years about that and occasionally tease me about that mean old chicken summer of of thirty eight This could have contributed to the fact that she had a hard time convincing me to get into that well bucket to go down into the well to remove the dead snake a year or so later.?maybe!!after the chicken thing, I was not too sure the snake was dead, I mean it was possible, I had seen lots of snakes that lived in the water, and that made me hesitant, could mom be wrong again?but in I went, and that time she was right. whew__!!

FIREWOOD 1937-1941

Wood cutting was a man's job, in the early fall dad and and my uncle would go into the woods with saws and axes and cut down large oak trees these were a hardwood tree that when dried would burn hot in a fireplace and moms stove, there were two different kinds of oak trees white oak and red oak both were favored as excellent heating material after the trees were cut down they were sawed into fireplace length and hauled back to the house, and cut in half again and split with an axe into stove wood for the cook stove, if the area that the wood was sawed up, back in the woods was not suitable to get the wagon into then a sled was used to get it home to the woodpile after it was considered that we had enough for the winter, dad would help my uncle gather his firewood for his winter supply. This usually started in the month of October and continued until some time in November if weather permits, working together seemed to get the chore done faster.

Then the splitting of the huge logs begin. Dad used an Axe when possible and at times had to use a sledgehammer or a maul and a large steel wedge driven into the wood to split it, some of the Hickory and white oak were very hard dense grain wood.

It was necessary to split it up so it would dry faster and easier to stack into the wood shed and it was also lighter in weight for me and my mom to carry into the house, O yes I got lots of "Bring in the "firewood" duty every day.__ some of it was still quite heavy so One day I decided to split it up a little more. I had watched my dad do this for hours at a time so I know how its done. _ yep__ 5 minutes later using my dads big double bit very sharp Axe right through my shoe and my big toe on my left foot I split it to the bone laid it wide open. Poor mom! Dad was gone helping my uncle do his wood cutting. So we were all alone, and about ten miles to the doctor. And dad was on the mule.so walk was our only option, or run around in the woods trying to find dad. She finally got it to stop bleeding and tied it up in some rags and gave me an aspirin. When dad came home,_ days later I was hobbling around in the house with my whole foot wrapped up and a sock on it to keep it from becoming infected, lots of red hot "Iodine" used back in those days, keep it from becoming infected. no phones, no help, you were own your own, desolate, and helpless so mom did what she had to do, keep the bandage tight. I had a real problem walking and the bleeding had almost stopped, by the time dad came back home, the next problem was how to get me to school I had already missed a week of school, so mom put a blanket on the mule and I rode old "Kate"the mule to school until about the Thanksgiving holidays and I could walk again. I Still had a problem wearing my shoes, and that one one was ruined, I still got that scar, but that incident stopped my wood splitting days. Dad took that over again. And I went back to watching the wood being cut and split Mom didn't mind, neither did I. Cutting and Splitting wood was for me very dangerous!!! In1940.

Example 1946

I had a lot and I mean a lot of cousins some older and some my age some younger my mom's family were visitors, more so than my dad's not as much of course because they were spread out all over everywhere one was my uncle in Savannah Ga Another, uncle up in New Jersey another, uncle in the Navy, that only left my aunt that was in Ga. at least she had one girl my age we were in the same grade in the grammar and high school and the only difference between us was she was quiet and smart and getting an education and I was neither,, I seemed to constantly be getting into trouble, big difference. Same school. What's the problem here? Not one male teacher in that school why? Lotta boys in that school and they definitely all had trouble.Not as bad as I did but I still think they used me as an example to the rest of the boys.and I guess it worked, up to a point I don't know, I got out of there, not the easy way, but for me the only way just just like a bad dream. O. Lucky me. Another Puberty problem was with girls, not the ones at school, most of them were really cool, mostly well behaved girls, some were a little rough but were easily intimidated compared to me and some of the other boys there at the time in school.

It was those kissing cousins of mine that bothered me most, I hated going to see some of those girls there was three of them that we visited on a semi regular basis and I never felt safe around these, they wanted to kiss, kiss, kiss, I don't think they had any limits and wouldn't keep their hands to themselves.I guess aggressive girls was not my forte they are more like boys are portrayed by some people and I can sympathize with some of the girls but after all these girls were my relatives, and I was nervous around, some of them. I never knew what they were planning to do to me next.

It was kinda Scary to be fondled By a girl I was not a piece of meat Right girls? And I was not excited about it actually was an embarrassing situation for me I had never experienced it before and for a cousin to do it was even more of a shock than a turn on in my instance, But I lived over it, and never hurt anyone's feelings that I know of and I only let them go so far though.!!! I did have to threaten to tell on them to get it stopped they treated me bad afterward and it was strange, feeling, I didn't want to go there anymore to even visit them.

Home town hero's

In my home town we had 2 famous people that lived there one was before my time but I'm still glad I got to know him, NAP was our water commissioner for the city and a very famous Baseball left hander He pitched 6 shutouts one year and led the National League in pitching 27 complete games a great baseball player "he used to play for the Dodgers and coached our little sand lot baseball team back then and we learned a lot from him of course none of us little guys knew who he was and he never told us about his career in the game, he was about sixty two at that time, we were just too young to have known about him. He was born in a little area just north of my hometown Called Crabapple,. My dad was a big fan of his and he also knew Ty Cobb and I remember going to visit him with my dad but I was only six or eight at that time and baseball was not important to me at that time. But my dad was a big baseball player back when he. Was a boy

JACK. 1957---1962

Later in my teens there was a NASCAR race driver that was my hero that lived in my hometown "Jack Smith" he won a lot of races from fifty seven to sixty two drove Pontiacs it was the thrill of my life and he knew it!! To be hitchhiking and have Jack stop and pick us up, some of my buddy's would not ride with him as we usually went in twos when hitching a ride _ but I did!!! And he use to try to scare me He had a forty Ford two _Dr that was fast!! I had seen him drive a race car and I loved it he could really tear the road to Buckhead up 80__90__100__ mph down the road and I'm smiling and hanging on.for dear life. my life life was. Complete to have that kind of a. Thrill riding with Jack Smith,, Get it!!!Jack Get it!!! I would yell as he would throw it into a slide, And he would smile! he knew that was a thrill For me!

I use to go to the garage where he worked on his car and help him sand the repaired dents in the race car before he painted it I liked hanging around his shop close to that race car, and much later when I was building my first "Dirt Track" car he gave me lots of tips and first hand information on how to set up the front suspension so it would turn correctly. He was kinda a quiet kind of guy about the races he won or lost and he was a very serious person no bragging just facts, about his car.I liked him.and he he was my buddy. My hero, my friend.

He was a hard worker but I hated it when he pinched my shoulder muscles God that hurt!!!.he was a strong man.and drove a car to win!!. That was his constant goal, and I'm so glad to have been able to know him as a person not just as a race fan. Except i sure wished he would not pinch my puny shoulder muscles,!and then laugh. I. Soon learned to run when he got close by.and he would laugh about that too.but he taught me a lot about bodywork and painting and hammering out bent fenders, and sanding, and sanding, and sanding, building up those shoulder muscles,! To drive that dirt tracker later on, those old cars did Not have power steering, you needed those strong shoulder muscles, then I knew!!! And I have pinched a few puny shoulders of some aspiring racers myself since, and laughed...they had no clue, and it would be years before they did!.Thanks Jack!!! It was great having the opportunity to just hang around and hug that race car with you.man.

NASCAR CHAMP 1957--1959

Another of my friends was Tim Flock he owned a Pure oi gas station over on Piedmont Avenue north Atlanta Tim "Owned Daytona "race track when they were still running on the beach, back in the fifties and drove those big Chrysler 300s and he was a winning driver, only about 5 ft 4 and thin built, but a fierce competitor in a race car, of that no one doubted. He was champion material.

And had a co_ driver for a while__ A monkey___ Jocco Flocko!__ Tim was a lot of fun to talk to, he had some really tall tales to tell, he was the youngest of the Flock Brothers And all the rest of his family tried to stop him from driving a race car he said, but he was determined and was a great one, all his brothers drove race cars and his sister was no slouch behind the steering wheel either, they were all from over in Alabama real close to the Ga. Border. And at the Flock Bar Down in Atlanta you might see anyone of NASCAR "Greats" there at anytime___ had a few brews there myself. Later when i was old enough, Fonty and Bob showed up sometimes.the older brothers were great drivers also!. But were usually out racing up north in a different racing circuit than NASCAR.it was the most popular in the south.at that time. My Dad built some nine inch Ford rear ends for Fonty for for his race cars in fifty five, he was racing racing up north in the Midwest racing asso. circuit then.

Daytona was my thing every year and no matter what, I always found a way to get there with someone, somehow, back when they raced on the beach, sneaking in was easy if you were not afraid of those palmetto Diamondback Rattlesnakes that ran loose in the area. Seen some of those that were six feet long and fat. All you had to do was get there, sleeping on the beach was allowed in the old days, But as usual the drunks ruined that plus some of the idiots got ran over laying on the driving area of the beach. Moonshine runners were some of the best racers one of the best was Roy Hall but Roy didn't follow the rules too often and NASCAR couldn't do much with him so they barred him from racing with them. all them "good ole boys" were a lot of fun to hang out with. Back in those days.and sure knew how to drive a race car. And I got to visit "THE BEST DAMN LITTLE GARAGE IN TOWN" Smokey himself That alone was worth the trip I know that my dad wanted to go also but duty prevailed and I'm sure he worried about me but I was a footloose and fancy free kid in those days.School would wait Daytona only happened once a year.!!.at that age I fancied a racing career for myself someday.I had the nerve and the skill but just didn't have the money. Or the connections to get started, there are a lot of Jeff Gordon's and Jimmie Johnson' out there driving Taxis and Bread trucks that only need the chance to become great..The early.fiftys were exciting and trying times for me!!! But these guys were my hero's and good ones too.

GONE FISHING 1949

Now fishing is one of my fun time things to do__I think it was in forty nine Labor Day weekend the first time that dad and I went to Florida to go deep sea fishing, the Town was Carabelle Fla. its on the Gulf side of Florida about half way up the coast it was then a sleepy little fishing town and we went out on the "Cavalier" the captain's name was Earnest and the deckhand said just to call him "Knuckle Head" so we did, that was dad's first case of seasickness and he had it bad, I was not real far behind him, but I got to catching some Red Snappers that were about twenty lbs and forgot about it, after dad saw some of the catch, he rallied and began to get his share of them, we had a great fish story to tell back home, we came home with three. five gallon cans full of filleted fish and friends and neighbors shared the bounty. We went back several times in later years and always brought back great amounts of fish. those were some of my favorite fishing trips and a few years later I went down there and went out on a commercial fishing boat mostly for the experience and it certainly was that, They don't come back to port until the boat was full and on that trip it was five days you fish at the rail one hour on then one hour off twenty four hrs_ at a time no sleep, when the fish are running in a school and the catch is fast and furious, and this system catches lots of fish, then we move to another area(that's when you sleep if you are smart) then back to the same routine _ I thought the boat bottom had fallen out it took days and nights to fill this boat and head back into port __ my pay for this trip was almost four hundred dollars but I would never ever do that again I had to get a motel room and sleep about thirty hours to be able to drive back home to Georgia, never again! That's one time that I got enough fishing to last me a long_ long_time!!!.now that's fishing. Those guys are Real fishermen, I'm just a worm drowner compared to them i'm a novice.

Chattahoochee River 1948-1949

Other fishing trips involved camping out overnight with some of my summer friends down on the Chattahoochee river not too far from the home of a sweet young girl in my seventh grade class that i liked a lot, should have hooked up. with her when i had had the chance. Usually on weekends which required permission from at least my mom who would then clear it with my dad we usually fished with "throw" lines, these are hooks tied on to a strong cord and baited with some foul smelling pieces of long dead chicken and a heavy piece of metal (usually a worn out plow point) these were thrown out into the river as far as possible by the strongest one among us and the slack taken up and then fastened to a tree or strong bush. We would usually put ten to twenty of these out at about one hundred feet apart we were fishing for the Blue Catfish or as some called them "Channel cats" they grew up to sixty lbs if you got a big one. And upon a rare occasion we caught them. but not that big. about a ten pounder looked really big.

One of us had to go out close by and hopefully borrow a nice fat chicken to roast over the fire, While we sat around the fire and smoked cigarettes and tell lies about our hopeful, and mostly non existent sex lives, mostly about our almost, sex conquests our ",how would that be" sex lives!!! And which one we dreamed about, the most, kinda like a wishing contest for each one of us lying our ass off to each other trying to stay awake.

And then go run the throw lines, to do that we go and hold the line in our hand and see if anything is pulling on the line, if so we pull it in an take off the catch re bait it and throw it back in if we all don't go to sleep we run the lines about every hour or so._ most of the time we fished from Friday night until Sunday afternoon and then split up the catch and go home for some real food and help clean the fish for a fish fry Sunday night.back at home, we usually got some nice big ones to take home, If our parents were ever worried about us we never knew it, I can't remember them ever coming down to look us up while we were there along that big wide dangerous River. I don't remember anyone getting drowned or missing on the river.we were just boys doing what boys do back then in Georgia back in forty eight.

Huck Finn & Tom Sawyer would have loved it. We were real river rats back then and enjoyed ourselves swimming and fishing and, getting tan We aso had a boat made from two wrecked forty six Chevy hoods cut off square at the back and welded together with three seats of wood and a homemade paddle it looked similar to a canoe and cost us about five bucks total for the welding, used it for years down on the River. Painted it kinda a mud color, that made it easier to hide, I think one of those big floods finally washed it away, one spring it was gone, It took us all together to come up with a whole five bucks to pay for the welding About three weeks,, real money. Was scarce in those days.!!! And it washing away was a great loss to us, we never had another. Had to build a raft from scrap lumber from a old barn, it was hard to control and it became waterlogged and sunk on us one weekend, We just gave up!!! and borrowed a real boat after learning how to pick the lock on the chain it was tied up with.

We always put it back where it came from and did no damage to it, nice aluminum boat.we even filled the. Gas tank sometimes five gallons was about a. Dollar.

No clue 1947

Cotton picking time was usually hot and humid time of the year and help finding people that knew how to pick it was a problem, so kids were hired to pick also, in forty seven there was a measles outbreak and also the mumps were going around also so I and my brother both caught the measles first and a few weeks later the mumps, just as I was recovering from them I got a phone call at home from a man that I had helped pick his cotton the year before, he had been trying to remember my name and finally did, wanted to know if me and my brother would come over and pick the "scraps". Of what was left of his field of cotton now scraps are what is left after the first heavy picking is finished and the slow to open boles have opened Its a cool blustery day in October and i just was almost over the mumps, but he said he was paying double wages to get the fields stripped of cotton, so my brother and I slipped out the bedroom window and went over and picked cotton until almost dark, my mom was out of her mind, worried and then furious with us for being out all day just out of the bed with the mumps, out in the cold wind all day picking scrap cotton, but we made a whole dollar each mom!! Look and showed it to her and she sat down in the kitchen and started laughing and crying at the same time and my brother and I were at a loss trying to understand why that she was happy and sad at the same time???

Mothers? Hard to understand them, going to kill us one minute and laughing and crying the next,.. No clue...at the time.

Fall 1939

Hickory nuts fell off the trees in the fall of the year, if it was a good year for the trees they were plentiful but the squirrels really loved them so you had to really be aware of when they would start falling it was amazing how my mom knew exactly when it was time to go hickory nut hunting but she did. it was on a Saturday after lunch that we all got an old five lb lard bucket and headed for the woods,,_ Hickory trees grow profusely in the south the squirrel does his thing and buries the nuts and they forget where and the nut sprouts and nature does the rest the problem is it is a slow growing tree but they tend to be kind of in groves and the wood is very hard and durable_ lots of the old country beds and furniture are made of Hickory wood hard long lasting hickory wood.

After a few hours we had our buckets full of the nuts and home we go then the fun begins cracking the nuts with a hammer and using a bobby pin, hair pin, what ever you call it, picking the "meats" out of the nuts that takes at least a full day for the three of us with the other chores that have to be done to finish the picking of the nuts now the good part after all this aggravation with the. nuts mom bakes a cake and puts bits of the meats in the batter Now we know why the squirrel loves Hickory nuts so much, Yes it's a lot of bother but the cake is_SO GOOD!!!! And we worked so long to get it and its kinda like Christmas it only comes once a year. If there was a great harvest we would keep lots of the nuts and get two cakes a year another benefit of being a country boy, in the country.

City folks don't know what they missed.!!!.its also too bad hickory trees don't grow out west I would love to bake another of mom's hickory nut cakes. Another tree that disappeared in my mothers time was the chestnut trees, she used to tell us about hunting and gathering the chestnuts when she was a little girl, and how her mom put them in a large pan and roasted them in the wood stove oven. She said some type of beatle came thru the chestnut trees and eventually killed all of the large trees.and she missed them.And at times about Christmas they were available in a grocery store, and mom would. Get a bag of chestnuts to roast for herself, Another nut we roasted and boiled a lot was the peanut. We grew them on the farm also, up in the last rows of the garden, no matter how many we had we never had enough, seems the more we planted the more we ate. Mom would roast them in the oven, and boil them with salt and homegrown peppers. We ate them hot and hotter. We also made our own peanut butter and sometimes made peanut "brutal" it was supposed to be brittle, but if it cooked a little too long it made it "brutal" to eat it was so hard, it was still good, candy from the store was not in the budget, not in 1939 and not many people would barter goods for candy or cokes, those were cash money items not necessity items mom said. She made lots of sweet things for her kids.

Rationing 1942---1945

During ww two almost everything was rationed and depending to the size of the family as to how much you were allowed to get anything, also at times things were only available on certain days this made grocery shopping quite a chore you had to plan wisely what and when to order your supply, in those days your groceries were delivered to your home by the store, gasoline was rationed, also none of us except dad could drive the car anyway and different classifications were to be had for gas if you were a defence worker (working at a company that produced war materials) you were allotted more gas than most others, but that had to be conserved no gas for joy riding, peanut butter, jelly, meat, fruits, milk, butter, and lots of canned goods were not available at times beer, whiskey, all this and more not available at all this created the so called Black Market for hard to get items at very lucrative prices on some low grade products. Auto tires were especially hard to get and only after a long wait, auto parts also a long wait.

Most people grew a "Victory Garden" in almost any space that could be found to produce food for your family, those were "lean years" every thing for the "troops" was the motto! The need was great on the home front, but the war needed everything and we all gladly accepted that fact and adjusted our lives accordingly. The Nation was as One in those days, we were the "United" states of America in forty five. I was eleven when the war ended, and the boys started coming home, our factories had to switch back to civilian markets no autos had been built since forty one and most people were driving junky old cars and a great boom in all products was needed by the people! Returning men wanted wives and homes and kids. We lost my mom's father in forty seven also president Roosevelt back in forty five and that's when we got "Truman".

Wild about Harry 1945

"The Buck Stops Here" Harry S. Truman for president, I grew up in the great "Need Era". Money was still a problem and jobs were available and the FHA was started up, the banks were making car and home loans, some of the auto manufactures were financing auto loans and funds were made for returning men to buy new homes with low cost loans, by forty eight our people were almost back to normal. But there were still big "Shortages" of almost everything. Good times were on the way in forty nine into fifty one, until Korea. Why is it always too good to be True!!! I wondered?

Allen Road 1942--1946

The spring of 1942 we moved to a nice house on Allen rd. The school there I did not like but the neighbors were good the neighbors to our east were older couple that had a granddaughter that was mentally handicapped some way, and was about thirteen years old. At that time I had never seen or been around anyone like her, she lived there with them, and they had fenced in the complete backyard for her, my mom told me that she runs away if she gets out of the yard, she also pulled off all her clothes and ran around and around the yard naked. She was a pretty girl with beautiful red hair when she did this I would go tell my mom and she would call her grandmother and tell her about that and her grandmother would take her into the house. Then one day my mom sat me down in the kitchen and told me they she died last night! O No!! She could not talk, but she use to hold my hand thru the fence and smile at me, I remember going outside and into the toilet and crying my eyes out, the next day was Sunday and her grandfather also died, mom said of a broken heart. I remember they were both in caskets in the living room on Monday or Tuesday when mom and I went over to pay our respects, and I cried some more, I was so sad for her, she lived but, she never had a life.

That was really sad and poor lady lost her granddaughter and husband in only two days. Mom was very sad also visited us almost every day after that, mom said she was lonely and made us stay outside.

On the other side to the west was a family with four kids only one at my age a girl the youngest of the four she was ten I think, and I was close to ten or eleven also, I had to play with her because her brothers wouldn't, she was too silly they said, so I learned to play house with her, we built our house way back in the woods behind our house we had seven acres there so plenty of room and mom never seemed to care where we were, when she called

I always answered her, most of the time she just wanted to know where I was, she and I became playmates, so this particular day I had to pee, so I just stood up and went at it and we went back to playing, a few minutes later she wanted to see that thing I had, so kinda reluctantly I unzipped my pants and showed it to her, big mistake.

She knew more about what to do to with it then than I did, her brothers liked it she said, and so did I, so it became a regular thing over in the playhouse, she said she did it to all her brothers, all the time at night, she thought nothing of it. And I have to say that she was better at it than I was. It was a new thing to me live and learn we moved from there in forty six and I never found another girl like her until I met the California girl in forty seven over at the swimming hole.

I had a swim suit but it was more fun without it! Just showing off.!!! She certainly knew what excited boys and how to, and what to do to them, and she was better at it than any other girl and showed me how and where to be very gentle, and also do it to her! Wow, Now that was also something new to me but it made her so intense, and sometimes it made her cry, but it didn't hurt she said, but it scared me a girl thing I thought??

I didn't really know much about that, or girls at that time. But I liked them a lot!! And I liked being with them, it was a nice feeling, and they smelled so good. And it made me have funny feelings in my tummy when I was with them. And I liked that! And I liked her also.

Green Grass 1946

About the summer of forty six I saved enough money up from my grass cutting business ect. to buy a bike at the five and ten cent store and now I got "wheels" everything speeded up, things got done faster, I even got a pair of roller skates ten cents more for the skate key. So as far as my grass cutting went I expanded it to more people and more $ poor mom, she never knew where I was, I was just out working, there was a lot of people building houses, making good wages but didn't have time or the energy to mow the grass, my specialty.

I even had a rubber stamp made in North Atlanta for two bucks and with a ten cent ink pad made my own business cards they were a little crude, but they had my home phone number on them, I found out later that I should have cleared that with my mom first though, she was not my secretary and almost put me out of business, but with a little whining and sniveling she caved in and took messages for me. I think she really got to enjoying it because some of my customers started telling me what a nice mother I had after talking to her on the telephone, she ask if I was doing a good job and that how much I enjoyed doing it for them. She was just "Bragging me up" to them, it was kinda embarrassing for me, but she was my mom after all and I would buy her something she wouldn't buy for herself at times like a new apron or hairbrush and she always said the same thing when I did, ``Aww now you shouldn't have done that `` but i wanted to do something nice for her after all she had gotten dragged into the grass cutting business whether she liked it or not and I can only imagine what would have happened had we had cell phones and riding lawn mowers in those days!! WOW!!! Lotta Green Green grass in Georgia in in the summer time.

Dad would have wanted to know where I stole the phone and mower and beat my ass if I didn't own up to it. Tough life growing up back then in forty six and it was against the law for me to get caught with any money at all. We were taught to beg or barter for it from mom, she made sure we earned it by giving us a lot of yard work to do before any dimes were handed out to us kids for any reason, especially the movies.

The Enforcer1946

My mom always said that she was kinda like a "tea kettle" most of the time she was cool and at times would kinda simmer but before she boiled over she whistled, so everyone could get out of her way, ha ha, and I think that was close to describing her, very very well. My parents didn't fuss, argue, or fight no cursing swearing, or insulting each other.

My dad was Man Of The House mom always said and he was the Enforcer right or wrong rare for her to voice an opinion in front of us kids about any punishment to be dealt out on us kids, dad however did not, that I remember ever raise a hand to our sister Sandra, she did no wrong! That evidently fell to mom to handle as she saw fit, if it ever happened we boys were not allowed to witness it. That was another subject that was never brought up and at times I swear she turned red and had horns!!! She loved ratting us boys out to get us in trouble, I didn't think we were that mean to her, although there were time!!! If she had not been injured by being hit that Sunday morning by that car we (us boys) would have tied her to a tree back in the woods and left her. We loved her but for a while she was a real Brat.

Kid Brother 1946

My kid brother would get mad at me about something and run to mom swearing that I had hit him in the stomach so hard that he could not breathe and gasping for air (faking it) perfectly, and mom would jump me and sometimes use the broom on me two hours later just when he was not expecting it I got even yep hard to the stomach "Now go tell mom about that"!! I had to stop that when he got about six foot two tall. He was bigger than me took after my mom's side of the family, Those 7 Foot German Giants. I kinda took up for him in school but in our late teens, nineteen or so that became his job for me!!

BUGS 1946

Georgia is a beautiful state it has almost everything from sea shores, beaches, swamps, plateaus hills, mountains, rivers, large lakes every thing but deserts, at one time we even had lightning bugs this little guy was a slow flying bug with a lighthouse in his rear end that blinked off and on just after dark at night (about the time the snakes came out) we use to catch them and place them in a jar and use them for a night light sitting on the window ledge after going to bed. mom would sneak in after we were sleeping and pour them out outside so we could catch them again the next night, over and over!!I'm not sure if they are there anymore, too many kids so few lightning bugs, maybe all gone by now. The north Ga. Mountains were rich at one time in trout and other game fish. We always had ole "whiskers" (catfish large and small) in the rivers and lakes all over Ga. Nothing any better in Georgia than Catfish and hush puppies on on a Saturday night at home with every body digging into them, mmmm good.

My dad and his friends and some of my uncles use to go "Grabling" in the rivers for fish and turtles this was a technique where they stuck a foot and leg back underneath the river banks to find fish or turtles hiding there then diving under to pull them out sometimes a big ole water moccasin snake sure made us kids run, if it was a fish or turtle we then place them in a burlap sack called a (tote sack) and depending on how many were caught, the fish were fried up and eaten and some of the turtles were tied up to keep.

By the leg with a wire and kept in the creek and fed until eaten, we had two distinct turtles one was the large "Snapper" mean ole rascals, and the other was the "soft shell" these usually found buried up in the sand bars along in the river bends and all you needed was Stealth and an old broom handle or good strong stick to pin them down with and put them in a bag to carry home better than chicken all white meat like frog legs and this was something mom would tell my brother and I when we were going over on the river for our fishing trips when we were nine and twelve years old You Boys Bring Me back two or three of them soft shells if you can and lots of times we did. We knew how to get those on a sandbar, with a stick.

Flying 1940

I can still remember how disappointed I was the day I had on my cape like Superman and jumped off the chicken house trying to fly I hit the ground hard and it knocked the air out of me and I laid there on the ground crying more out of disappointment than injury that was the first time that I realized that some of the things that I believed in were not in fact true you can't fly! That hurt in more than one way, I don't remember how old I was at that time, but I was old enough to stand in the drug store and look at comic books and believe that I could fly.

And the day I soloed in my little Cessna 150 in seventy one and even later in my life I flew all over the west and and in old Mexico, that thought again ran thru my mind as I looked down on the runway below it brought a quick little smile to my face I can fly! like my mom always said "you got to try." There was no TV in my life until I was about twenty years old. We had comic books and the radio to keep our imagination alive and growing, as soon as I got home in the fifth grade it was to the radio and thirty mins. of Sky King, The Green Hornet, Superman, Roy Rogers, The Lone Ranger, and all the comic book hero's, and homework and after that was done, my afternoon chores to be done, chickens to feed and water, then feed the hogs bring in the kindling and coal in the winter, check the kerosene can, and refill moms stove tank, help mom in the kitchen to get supper table set because dad liked to eat soon as he was home on the 7:10 bus.

By 8:30 its time for bed or your whipping for whatever the offence today was, then at 9:00 to bed school day tomorrow up at

5:00 am light the oil cook stove, in the fall and winter build a fire in the heater, get my bath, moms up, dads up, breakfast and off to work for dad at 7:00 am bus everyone's up off to school at seven school first bell at eight am until three thirty Schools out home by four, and it all starts all over again. Some life huh? Wintertime I ran my rabbit boxes to check for rabbits between five and six killed and skin them and hang them on the clothesline to dry or freeze after washing it really good and try to be at the market to sell them for ten cents each by seven thirty am then on to school. Every day!!! So any type of excitement was a break in the boredom!! Spring was a welcome time Summer even better. Good times are back again, snake bites, hornets, swimming, fishing, grapes, watermelon, chiggers, BlackBerry's, fun time!!!!! yeyaaaaaa!!! No school in the good ole summer time....

The next summer after my poor start with a large retail store and after working in the ice cream dept at ice cream plant last summer I got a job with them again as an ice cream T G man the T G trucks were the ice cream man the cute little trucks that drive slowly thru your area with the music box playing little kiddy tunes, that make little kids of all colors crazy wanting a popsicle or a fudge bar those were only five cents the T G or Triple Goodness bar were ten cents ice creams on a stick your kids favorites!

I loved this job! I gave away almost as much as I sold, lots of little kids, or their moms had no money, so the Popsicles had two sticks I would split them in half and give it away to the little ones with no money, but when I became a regular guy every day about the same time mom found a few cents for her kids treats. A lot of the moms came down to the truck to thank me for giving to her child so they would not feel left out and stand around crying while the other kids had their ice treats, it was just not right I thought.

This happened a lot over in the colored sections of Atlanta and also some of the poorer sections in the white areas I gave away a lot of Popsicle's to a lot of kids, I became very popular in all the areas of my route I usually sold three truck loads per day as versus most of the other drivers two and my route was supposed to be in the poorer section of town, my last run thru my area was about ten pm until midnight on the really hot days, lots of older people too hot to sleep and a pint of good cold ice cream just hit the spot! Sitting out on the front porch cooling off. This job was a summer job only but I averaged about seventy five to eighty five dollars per week commission which was more than the other drivers, but they were afraid to go into my areas at night I never had any type of problems. Day or night!!! Some of the older ones remembered me from my stove wood and shine days when I was just a kid, and often invited me up on the porch to have ice cream with them, and talk about our day.

Lots of good folks over in those areas just like me Poor but Proud!!! And if they didn't have any money that was OK black Or white, I was happy to share, three quarts would usually do the job nicely, my treat and thanks, was payment in full. Little did I know that I was going to meet my sweet thang, my future wife Margaret on my ice cream route, but I did.

Q. time1949

Sometimes Saturday nights were so boring that we didn't want to see the movie here in town so as we kinda moped about until someone come up with an idea of some Barbeque! Well the best was about thirty miles away unless you wanted the local from down in the black section of town and they were usually sold out by dark, yes it was that good.

So now we had to ante up the money and count to see if we could afford to get there and back with the food, and some of these guys could really "Hide some Groceries" the money was pooled and some times we could come up with thirty or thirty or so dollars so gas was bought or borrowed from someone's car via a

Ga. Credit card and we are on our way out to the Bankhead ave. "Q "just east of the river in west Atlanta Bankhead Ave. Area.

Now this was also Forbidden Territory to us hillbilly's the boys over in that area had sent out "Not Welcome" messages to the crew, we were, cutting in on their action with some of the very friendly girls over in that area and several of them had "gone for a ride" with some of us, but we were a cocky bunch and a good butt kicking was no stranger to most of us, So four car loads of us headed out some of the bunch were old enough to buy beer and a six pack cost from seventy five cents for Krueger cream ale and up to a dollar for Blue Ribbon, so it was in the budget with the "Q" we were there about four six packs before the locals showed up. Some of the girls were there already with us and drinking our beer and smooching with us, but we were about twenty five strong and they only had eleven so it was "Friendly", and we all joined in together boys and girls and had a good time.

and they all decided that us "Hillbillies" were not such bad guys after all, we had money, paid for our own food and drinks, treated the girls with respect,. and we went out there many times after that with no problems and "took several girls for a good ride" at least they liked us. Some of the boys.came to our town with revenge on their minds, but they found out quickly about our hometown girls, now they understood why we were over there. Our town was Dry.completely Dry!!! Big Time Dry!!!.That darn drought again.no hot girls walking around our town. --0 --Nada. none.

The summer that I drove the T G ice cream truck I lived in Atlanta, and I kept that quiet from my Juvi. Visits on my monthly reports, they might have taken offence, because of the fact that next door to where I lived at the Hotel and my dad worked for a large truck rental company they had transferred him to this location a large night garage located on the same street about ten miles from the main ice cream plant up in northern Atlanta, I parked my T G route truck there also at night when I came in, It was a plug up area for my unit, It was very hot that summer and i had to drive up to the main plant every A M to refill my morning load at nine am or :until about noon when I started my route.

My uncle and aunt were not too happy with the new way I wanted to be able to stay in town so I could work more hours therefore making more money, but they were responsible to the juvenile court for my welfare and dad worked next door at night and he was known not to be too happy with me, but everything worked out great.when I brought my truck iron. For the night about one am in the morning and plugged I up, dad and I talked, he was surprised at how much money I made each day, and sometimes, I would slip him a twenty to give to mom, we never had a problem.

JULIE 1950

After loading out my first load each AM I stopped off at a small park and watched two girls playing tennis I was not too familiar with this game, but they made it look easy as i was watching the game, I wanted to try it but was terrible when i tried to play it, and lots of laughing was done by us all as i tried to play. I gave them some ice cream, and talked.

They were both eighteen and seniors in school, I knew, they only played on Tuesday and Thursdays but Julie said she would meet me here every ten am if I wanted to learn to play tennis,, the other girl was not too friendly with me and often left the other girl and I early and went away. She said that the other girl was a virgin and was no fun, that puzzled me a little at the moment but I didn't reply. While it was early in the day, some mornings were really humid and the exercise was fast and furious with the game of tennis and I had a very hard time trying to keep up with her, and falling down, and behind on the score, she was more than good, no matter how I tried she beat me badly at this game every day, it was fast and faster. I often got very hot and sweaty and badly beaten at the game, by the time I had to start my route, wow!!! tennis was a real workout at the rate she played fast and hard __, and I was required to wear a white uniform on the job so I would shower in the little club house there at the court, and change from my tennis shorts and top into my uniform. For work.

One Friday morning as I was showering, I got the surprise of the summer when of all people that I could have imagined that would ever step into the shower with me it was a Visit from JULIE. she stepped into the shower completely nude I really did not know if what I was seeing was real. she said __"wash your back if you wash mine!!"___! Now I needed a reply, but didn't have one, and could not come up with one that would sound sensible__ so I turned around and backed up a little, I was also not in control of another "item" further down my body! She was a drop dead gorgeous girl, and nude even more so. and i did a slow sensual back rub on her backside while I tried to regain some self control over my body functions and thought process, in that short period of time, I failed, and she was_laughing and my mind was racing in an entirely different direction And when she took the soap and kinda turned toward me she gave me a big smile.

As she "Noticed" my condition and laughed, again, and ask had i ever showered with a naked girl before and I finally stammered out, No! Not with anyone as beautiful as you, She then ask me if I had ever had sex with a girl, and now was no time to make up some things real quick but All I could do was shake my head __ no__ that I was a virgin____ to make a long story short, she taught me lots of other things I had only heard the the big boys talk about but never had the opportunity to try _Yep A brand new world just came into view for me! And lots and lots Of Other things, and tennis_ I got pretty good at both, before the summer was out.she said!! We met there even after the ice cream business was over for the summer, and she and I returned to school in the fall. "nothing serious" she said just having fun!!!!!.Wow__ Some

Fun I thought. I could have really gotten serious with her.!! Never saw her after that fall_

Thought about her millions of times! She was a person you could not possibly ever forget!. A very aggressive girl, great personality, intelligent, sexy, played tennis like a pro. She was definitely my kind of girl.!!! And I hated to let her get away and I never learned where she lived or where she went to school, I would have really loved to date her, but there was my girl back at my school, and I was pretty well committed to her. But she did turn my head.and taught me something new about girls that I had never considered before my encounter with her at the shower house and that was, that they were as capable of seducing us as boys as we were some girls, something new!!! And I think I like it lots!

LUCKY IN 1950

I guess I really was after all was said and done "Lucky" to be a country boy in that era Because most of the people that lived in the towns were "Stupid" even after a good education they never had the hard experiences that we had in real life situations out in the "make do" categories that we faced almost every day in some way, they didn't have the problem solving experience that we had to develop out in the toolies, we had to learn the hard way to make things work or find another way to accomplish the same thing.

And then there were Girls a total and complete mystery to be able to understand for someone not in constant contact with them_ moms exclude, most of the time at least in my case she was the boss that I grew up with moms and Girls were totally different in my mind. Girls were almost completely totally nuts!!! No matter what they said, they did not mean, and changed their minds from day to day about everything.!!!

She loves me_____ she loves me not!!! I'm the same guy I was yesterday!! Why not??? I never understood the hormone damage to our minds, I guess because Girls grew up faster than boys we were idiots to them also, I know that more than one had told me that I was "immature" so looking back from today I guess they were right!! Our hormones were more concerned with who was the strongest, the toughest, and the bravest, and added together added up to the stupidest!! At least to the more mature girls., Balls before Boobs__ was our theory, in our minds, it affected most of us boys in our early teens, and seemed to wear off slowly in some of us. after that.

Hormones 1949

A girl that I liked could have "ask" me to jump off the Chattahoochee river bridge In the winter time and I probably would have, but ten boys could Not thrown me off it!!! Does that make sense? Nope!!! Hormones!!_I don't know about the effects on girls growing up But I know about the effect it had on me!_once it was in full swing puberty was a rough and confusing time for me! Maybe if I had had a more protected and normal start in life, but the bullies, starting in the 3rd grade and the fact that we moved three times in five years I never developed any lasting friends, and went through 3 different sets of bullies in such a short period, and of course the poverty that influenced opinion's of not only my peers but my teachers, gave me an inferiority complex that I was not aware of, and gave me a bad attitude that affected me for a very long time. Before I outgrew it. My parents did not understand me either, so I was more or less alone to work it out for myself_by the age of fourteen I was a very angry aggressive young man, things had to change and they did__ for the worst.!!all hell broke loose!I blew up before I was sixteen_and my life changed.I had to be conquered or understood, luckily I found someone that understood, the Dr.at the Juvi. Detention center "The Shrink" in Atlanta was very aware of my problems, and why i was so aggressive at times, and ask a lot of Stupid question Change in latitude, forty nine.

I knew mostly what the problem was, I needed a change in latitude for a change in attitude, and after three weeks in juvi.i found it, My Uncle and a cooling off period over in Alabama and I really, didn't have much choice, I had to go to school the state. Required it until 16, and I really wanted that diploma.

__And it worked___!! All my problems were back in Georgia, this was a new page in my life, a new opportunity to be normal, if I knew what that was? I still had a lot of resentment inside, but I slowly lost it, or replaced it with new feelings, and new friends and the slow creeping feeling of homesickness set in. This was new also and I had no idea how to contend with it,_

_ so I played football with a passion, a mean, nasty, aggressive passion, and found a degree of accomplishment, and acceptance by my coach and teammates, for my aggressive behavior on the field., my first feeling of being important, or appreciated by anyone!!!for anything!!!I So I wasn't completely useless,, I was in "unfamiliar territory" I scored five touchdowns that season from the defensive linebacker position, Almost Hero status!!!.according to the coach. We won eleven of our twelve games that season, the coach credited me for five of the wins.and I was honored with the the MVP award. that fall, a great ego booster, I was black and blue all over, I hurt, and got hurt but I never told or complained about it, It was a very angry physical sport, and I worked out a lot of aggressions out on that field.

And today, looking back at my first sixteen of life, I can't believe how fortunate I was to have survived some of the things that occurred, the lackadaisical attitude I had about some very serious events that could have caused serious injury or even my death And I don't think my parents were aware of some of the chances I took, and survived without even a thought about concerns of danger or consequences for my actions. As a kid of sixteen I had dealings with some very dangerous men in some dangerous business dealings, the trade they were in, it was a closed mouth situation or else but was the. Easy part for me, And I was not fully aware of just how much danger was involved, I was only interested in The money, that was my only motivation, Luckily I was smart enough to keep it quiet......

Thanks 1950

I am a Survivor,_and I contribute a lot of that to the girls and women in my life, girls seemed more mature the voices of reason that created some common sense into my hard head, And none of it was planned by me I'm positive but by fate._and the grace of God!! The1930s__50s held some pleasant and unpleasant experiences for me and, lots of other children growing up at that time. It was not chosen by us to be born into this environment that existed at the time, but it was our destiny.to be there at that point in time to help make it a better world for our children, and those who followed.us in this cycle of life. None of us can be sure of a future at all, and certainly. not a bright and successful one. Life does not come with a guarantee of anything. Or any amount of time.and many twists and turns, all unexpectedly.

Georgia 1947

We had a lot of pine trees in my area of Ga. In forty seven Lots of pine straw that we used for different purposes around the farm, the pigs loved it for a bed in the winter, we used it in our potato hill to protect them from the cold, the chickens used them in their nest and in the summer we piled it high and wide in our cave, plus it was plentiful just for the taking _There was one snake that loved it in the pines also that was the one we called the "Coach whip". Instead of its real name, and a lot of people really believed that it would chase you and whip you_ but other people said it was the "Black Pine Racer" snake,

I'm not sure what its real scientific name was but it was really fast on pine straw, we tried many times to catch them and always failed_ They were so black that they almost looked like a real dark purple in the shade of the woods, But I did manage to catch myself one in a rabbit box one fall over in the pine woods. And I shook it up pretty hard before dropping it out on the ground, and then pinched it on the neck so it could not bite me "I thought" but it wiggled loose and bit me 3_4 times on my arm and hand before I threw it down and it got away.

I was afraid to tell mom I didn't think it was poisonous but it was a snake, so I stopped by the doctors office on the way to school and was late to school because he was not in yet, and after telling him what happened, and describing the snake he put some iodine on the bite marks, laughed at me, patted me on the back, and told me that maybe I should try to find something else to play with besides snakes,.that was my third encounter with the biting reptiles. And after that I gave them a wide berth. Still do!!

Schools out 1945

Schools out for the summer,!!! Was a word at the age of eleven in forty five for me and age nine for my brother that I think we all enjoyed immensely, and if the report card was favorable, and you got promoted to the next grade that meant that mom and dad were going to be favorable for a two week visit to my dad's parents, my brother and I got to go up in the real country actually a farm, now they were alone at the farm and we were a welcome relief to the daily tasks and routine for them because we wanted to help, also we broke up the daily routine for them, and they usually found us something that really did help them,.a plus for us was the hugs and attention we got from them was special!!

And we loved them dearly, and hated to leave, and after a lot of pleading and begging by all of us, including grandparents we sometimes got an extra week with them, it was the stories that they told us about our dad when he was a boy that intrigued us it was good to know that he got "it" also..ha ha!!grandma cooked some of her famous dishes, which pleased not only us cut also grandpa very much, he said we needed to come up to see them more often so he could eat much better.to which grandma.told him "that's its back to gravy and biscuits for you next week" and he frowned and shook his head, and ask if we could just spend the summer with them?

We thought they were serious. But later on found out that they were just "joshing us" as they called it.It was so good to spend time there with those two.and it was good for them also, they always seemed genuinely glad for our visit, they were very "Set" in their ways and we 2 certainly broke that up. We had some wonderful times there.with them, and looked forward to going up there in the summer every year.

Playing ball 1945

I never learned why back in forty five at Elementary school that fighting with other kids was the thing to do, and it carried on into high school __when at the ballpark on Saturday we would choose up sides and have a great time playing baseball, without the fights, same kids on Saturday that they were next Monday that wanted to fight about everything, it never made sense to me, and we all hung out in front of the drugstore and movie theater in town Saturday afternoon and night and we all got along pretty well until next week in school, was it the stress that the school put on us or what?whatever its cause it was contagious I named it "Schoolitus"seems most everyone was up tight and always on guard especially on behavioral matters, it was extremely hard to just be yourself, it was a stressful situation that some of us "ignored", and consequently branded us as Troublemakers, to put it bluntly, we didn't "conform" and that's when our problems began.

Dirty brain 1945

I look back now and it was more like "Brainwashing than as educational. All the teachers were women, and it seemed to be if you were a girl then everything went OK_ but if you were a boy___these old maid teachers hated us boys I honestly think they tried to make girls of us behavior wise, and were having a problem with it and I will always believe that __I __was used as an example for the enlightenment of the rest of the boys at the school.I still resent the fact that my years there supposedly to receive an education were completely wasted.The fact that I finally went to a real school at in East Point and finally got a three year education proves my point.we were treated as young ladies and gentlemen. With a curriculum that had our education in mind not our behavior, economic status,, or Religious background., Home town was a Bad experience for me more like a prison, than a school. With a couple of exceptions 5 th and 7 th grade teachers were good teachers they knew the difference between boys and girls behaviors.and adapted accordingly,

I don't think some of the older teachers could do that., they were still teaching to the tune of the *hickory stick"!!! Back in the last century, Not working. Well at all In the early to mid forties like it did back in their day....!! And me and several other boys at that time payed the price for it.I don't know how long it took to modernize the schools there but I hope that too many didn't get their education like I did. They just weren't keeping up with the times, when I was there.old habits were hard to break._And so was I.But my brain was thirsting for the education I needed to go out into the world and be successful. And I unconsciously resented the fact that I was in a war with these people trying to "rule me", not teach me. I got ruled at home!!! I Always was an independent little cuss!!!.still am.

The first 100 years

I like many other kids think that sixteen __would never come! Another eternity before eighteen shows up then on to the next hundred years before twenty one and I became a man!_ now is when time starts to speed up, a few months later its the thirtys__ then forty, Wow that was quick_! Now things really speed up fifty _ two weeks later sixties are here,_ and seems like overnight seventy__Now you retire and while you're sleeping one night you wake up and you are eighty__ and this is the difficult age, because you start to loose those near and dear to you and time slows down again giving you awfully lots of time to grieve and mourn the losses that have befallen you and time drags on and more and more of your family and friends go away, and you are forced to start planning your own demise___ you know it wasn't that long ago that I was having all those problems back in school_____ did I ever tell you about the time_____!!!!!_____ Hello God,_!!!___ yes but..well!!.. I can explain all that. If you can give give me about a hundred more years?

PRE. CIVIL WAR Homes 1946

In the town I grew up in there are i think are still five fine old pre civil war homes that were not burned by Sherman's troops on their march to the sea and are expertly kept in like new condition and the grounds are kept the same, all of them at the time I was growing up were not the showcase homes they are today, most of them had descendants of the original owners still inhabiting them and were not open for visitors____, however, the grape arbors were grown over from years of neglect and the vines were extremely over loaded with some of the best grapes to be found, and I spent many hours sitting on top of an arbor eating my fill of those fantastic grapes, at times I would fill a five lb lard can full and bring them home for the other kids that also loved them, there were four different varieties of them in town, and it seems that I was the only one raiding them, as I never got run off from any of the arbors, and carried off gallons of them to take home so evidently it was permitted or the owners did not care.mom made some fine jelly from them and we enjoyed them for years and years, I wonder if any of them survived?.

Beautiful homes, but at that time we (my kid bro) and I were more interested in the old C S A Belt buckles that were to be found down at the old burned out ruins of a southern uniform factory at the junction at Big Creek Dam, we used to dig thru the ashes and screen out the buttons and belt buckles from the factory that had the C S A on them, those goofy Atlanta people would give us a whole dollar for one of those old Buckles in forty six And some of the buttons, we had dozens of them hidden in the woods down by the Hy.111 spring where we washed them up for sale on Sunday afternoon in front of the bank downtown on a little folding table to the Atlanta tourist just out for a little ride.we thought they were nuts and they thought we were nuts to selling those artifacts so cheap. wish I had some of them back I know we didn't get them all and I wonder if anyone else ever discovered the location of that old factory. I guess that was the only industry that The General wanted destroyed that was all that he burned. The rest of the town was left intact. The old original town was a cotton mill town it consisted of two parts the old town is about a half mile south of the newer part "uptown" was to the north and downtown has the old original town square park, a road was finally built between the two and connected them in the late forties the old mill village and the company store,, and bank were down town along with the company funeral home, the cloth produced by the mill went up town to be turned into clothing at the new plant, it was called the "pants factory" when I was going to school then.and a large group of the ladies of the town worked there.The little town of approximate five thousand that I knew is probably closer to three hundred thousand by now it become some prime real estate in the last fifty years I wonder if the old swimming hole is still there. over on r the creek? Kathy and I in the swimming hole naked together, I wonder where she is today and if she ever thinks of me.? I know that her parents both were chemists and she was an only child at the time, and they worked for one of the big Cola company's in Atlanta, and only lived at any place for six or eight months, and was home schooled by her mom, and was left at home alone and that she was lonely., and very curious about everything including sexual things, and she knew more about it than I did. and she was into making "it "feel good for her, but wanted to learn that about boys and how to make "it" feel good for them also. So we traded our knowledge. Little as it was., and practice, practice, practice it was a great summer.!!! Learned a lot about how girls worked.___Small minds do small things, but we were still learning about experimentation of such things as that. At that age we were still innocent but interested in these things, one of the mysteries of adolescent life.

My first day of school my mom and I walked the long way around the dirt road(about 6 miles) to meet with my teacher a very large lady, and a very nice lady she loved children, that was in Sept.1939 I was only 3 months from being 6 and this was a concern of my mom's __ not a problem she was assured, however the long walk did concern my mom, so my dad developed a path through the woods behind our house to follow the Big Springs Creek up to its source the spring itself, and turn Right, then proceed up the hill to the school yard, only about 2 miles, much shorter, and for the next week or so mom met me on the trail at different places, and it soon became a normal thing to go it alone. I did this until the spring of 42 when we moved and I went to a new grammar School there, That___ was the beginning of my troubles with schools, until this School, I had never had a fight, or been accosted by another boy, a new and frightening experience was now happening to me, Because I didn't fight back, I was tortured and bullied beyond belief, my dad was working, and my mom was not familiar with this type of behavior when she went to School, or in my previous School she had no solutions to offer me except to inform my teacher of this, and I did and all that did was make it worse, finally the principal allowed me to leave five_ minutes earlier than others so I could have a head start,__ Those were terrible years for me.

CHEROKEE COUNTY 1940

Back when dad was a boy there were very few people living in the area that he and his family lived, miles in fact in some directions from anyone, and he by nature of necessity had to be a hunter and a gatherer to supplement the diet of vegetables grown by his parents.all small game was hunted and fish were also an important addition to the diet, when I was old enough to be quiet while with him when hunting, he told me some of his experiences with different types of hunting and stalking deer back then, in my hunting time all the deer had been hunted out during the depression, dad said that they were plentiful back then in the mid 20s and also agreed that they were almost if not completely gone by the fifties.

my brother and I spent a lot of time in the woods, and never saw one, there were reports of Bears, and Panthers in our areas but. we never seen any signs of those either, but squirrels and rabbits were plentiful. And on one of those squirrel hunts with my dad I learned "The Hard Way" not to pick up a squirrel after my dad had shot it with his 22 and it fell out of a tall white oak tree to the ground, not far from where he had me to sit and watch and signal him if I saw one on my side of the tree, Of course his yell of "Don't Touch It". Went unheeded and I was upon it in a flash with my foot_ and the teeth of that dead squirrel were still buried thru my shoe and to the bone in my big toe on my right foot. When dad finally got it off me.!!And after the Wailing and Screaming, created from the pain, we quit the woods, dad said they were all over in Alabama by now anyway! Now I assure you that after that I carried a pretty long stick to poke any poor dead squirrel after that, and I had to be told, When to go poke the squirrel by dad before it was done, Those Things Are Mean!!!

In forty six a five hundred lb. Black Bear was shot and killed over in the Mountain Park area about six miles northeast of town in someone's backyard, and it was paraded around the town that Saturday morning for everyone to see, and it was huge. It was finally parked in front of the Ford dealership for hours for pictures and passers by to gawk at. And I gawked at it!!.that was one really big Bear.!!!glad I never met up with him out in the woods with only my slingshot.!!!I'd still be running.....That bear use to visit my imagination some mornings before daylight while checking my rabbit boxes over in the darkness of the swamp, Giving me goose bumps.!!!....

The movies

Some scary things were passed around amongst us kids, the late show at the movies that my brother and I used to sneak out our bedroom window to go watch were pretty scary at the time at our age, and the other scary stuff was what happens in the graveyard after dark? No one knew, because they didn't hang out there to find out it was too scary that was taboo, I knew, I use to hide in the graveyard and rattle chains and, moan long and loud and scare the pants off those guys who walked by after dark, to me that just enhanced the ghost stories that flew around the town, my brother and I were usually behind those stories and we laughed our butts off at these guys.

Marietta was about eleven miles west of my hometown and at times had a movie I wanted to see so, I would hitchhike over there in the afternoon after seeing the movie in town and stay for the late show there, now at one am in forty eight not many people are there from my hometown so the odds of a ride is slim to not at all in getting that ride, but I had chanced it a few times, before, and usually lucked out, but not always, now those unlucky nights meant a very long and lonely walk, or as I did it "Jog" I would run until I tired then walk a while Jog a while and was usually worn out at about the halfway mark with not a car in an hour or two,

There was a cemetery along the road there and two or three of the graves had a full size marble slab that was so nice and cool, And after a five or six mile Jog was a welcome place to stretch out and sleep until the am traffic woke me, and I could get a ride into town, make it home before nine am before mom and dad woke up, Sunday A M was the only time dad got to sleep in all week, and I would crawl back into my bedroom window and sleep until someone woke me up for dinner. Never got caught in the five or six times I did it.

And I don't recall seeing or hearing any ghosts or demons there, at least if there were any they were very quiet and didn't disturb me at all, however it was very nice of them to allow me to get some rest there. I needed it. That only worked in the summer and was not recommend in wet weather.

Honey bees1942

My mom's dad had Bees since twenty one I mean grandpa had bees!! Millions of bees, about fifty hives at one time of course they were also the only bees for miles around, and as every farmer knows you can't grow corn, cotton or a garden without bees Grandpa was the most fearless of men, he could do anything with his bees they seemed to like him, but only him, On a Summer Sunday afternoon the year I was seven my first cousin Alton and

I were down by the hives and decided to play "cars" and got between two hives each, he was in front of me about two hives, and accidentally pushed one of them over, this evidently was not a forgivable offense to the bees, because they swarmed all over him and me we ran back toward the house, screaming our heads off, all the moms came rushing out of the house, and carried us around to the front porch away from the bees that continued to fly all about the back yard, the hives were about fifty yards below the rear of the house, My cousin had been stung hundreds of times, and I had gotten twenty or more, we were both in extreme pain, and I remember my grandmother using tweezers to pull out the stingers from my cousin first, because he had so many, For those of you that don't know about honey bees when they sting you they have just committed suicide, the stinger is barbed on the end and pulls out the tiny sac containing the venom from the bees body and they die. And if. You slap or press the sting area you push the venom into the stinger and into you, so the correct removal of so many stingers from a young child's body can mean the difference between life and death, and my grandmother knew this, so I waited not so patiently for quite sometime while his stingers were carefully removed, then I got my turn. He was a very sick little guy for a few days, but we both made it. And did not have to be told to stay away from the beehives ever again..but we marveled at our grandfathers ease with which he handled his bees, and watched as he handled a swarm of them hanging on a tree limb and raked them into a new hive without being stung at all it was a wonder to behold to our little young eyes, we thought he was the bravest person in the world. And he was a giant of a man to us already at 7+ feet tall!!

And what he could do with those mean old bees proved it to us two. It was fun to go to this grandpa, s house he had a twenty six T model Ford over in the car shed, and we pretended to drive it as far back as I can remember, not much danger of us getting it going, because it took my dad and grandpa an hour sometimes to make it go it had no windows, and I went on one trip in it when it was cold___Never ask again it was a warm weather car and made funny noises, my dad drove it most of the time because dad said that grandpa didn't know how to use the brakes, he just hit things to stop. We were not allowed to ride with. Him.according to mom.

The old car was sold at auction in forty two After my grandma died one of my uncles bought it for twenty five dollars and stored it for thirty years my cousin Marion inherited it when his father died, and he completely restored it in his basement to like new condition, I saw it there in ninety five he has since died and now his daughter in in possession of it, he also restored one of my uncles twenty eight Plymouth sedan(the same one my dad drove me to the doctor in when the copperhead snake bit me at age five) also to like new condition._ I hope she keeps them. They are priceless.

COPS 1948

Pranks, Back in forty eight to some people were hilarious to us boys about town and no one, not even each other were safe from them, most were harmless but looking back at today's rules and laws some would be considered felonies, almost in today's world. One of our favorites was to watch when the police would go to supper at night and the word traveled fast as to where, and when, they were eating, someone would go in and watch them while the rest jacked up the police car took off all the lug nuts holding on the rear wheels on, and replace the hubcaps, lower the car gently, and get lost.then one of us with a car would throw a "Brodie" in front of the Restaurant, And watch as they rushed to the car and at times manage to get in and start to drive off before it fell, at other times it fell as they got inside, or as the doors were shut. It really was not funny unless you were close enough to watch it happen and boy did they swear and yell out to us they knew we had to watch them or it didn't have the results we wanted, but it was dark and usually a lot of folks in town so we just blended in quietly as possible. I think the city finally bought a small floor jack for the car, so it could be restored quickly, so then we just took all the lug bolts with us and threw them up on the roof of the police station, so they bought a whole bag of them from the Ford dealer and kept them in the glove box, then we disconnected the battery cables or took the starter solenoid., and at times it would be chained to a telephone pole with about one foot of slack.

The car was a forty Ford with a few hot rod goodies under the hood, I think it was an old confiscated "white lightning" car, it was a fast one!!!.but most of us boys knew our way around a Ford, sometimes we just jacked it up and put blocks under the Axle housing so the rear tires were about one inch off the ground, all the Fords were the same height so we would cut ten extras just in case and hide them around town for future use. Nothing like coming out from the movies with your date of the night and your car won't move yep it happens!.

We. Also were known to use a "Georgia Credit Card" Occasionally on the Police Car if we had cause to go to Atlanta for a night on the town. For those of you that are not familiar with the term G C C that's a.forty two inch long piece of garden hose and a five gallon gas can. We also have been known to use it while they were sitting in the police car, it's very quiet!! And we all knew how it worked!! it also worked well in the Atlanta areas especially over in the well to do part of town over there it was called the "Robin Hood" Credit Card!!!and it was used extensively at times when needed, I got one of the new ones made of plastic when they became available, kept it for years, every kid in Georgia had one. Hence the name! My Brother got caught in Atlanta using his one night. I forgot exactly how that turned out. I don't think he wants anyone to know!

AW RATS 1946

RATS_ In forty six they were not small ones, Big ones that are fattened on our chicken feed sacked about ten inches long, they don't live too close to the food source, but moved over under our house in the barn, and under the feed shed They rarely ever show themselves in the daylight and feed at night, but they leave trails where they run at night and they multiply like__ well, Rats in the early summer and we had some, The first clue was a hole in one of the feed sacks and dad got one in the house, well the hole in the feed sack could have occurred during loading or unloading but there is some spilled out over the floor that was not here last evening at that feeding after a week or so there are 5_6 bags of feed with holes in them, now__

_ its trap time, now what type of traps? well I decided to get the steel trap the one that catches them on the trails at night, the other type was the bait type but these were very well fed already so I didn't think that was the way to get them, my brother Troy and I ran the traps every morning noon and four times in the afternoon before dark we bought ten traps at fifty cents each (mom financed the deal) and we caught eighty eighty-five very large fat wharf rats in the next two days, every one of us was surprised at that, but of course we had no idea that we were that infested, they sure loved that chicken feed, we eventually over the next month took over over a hundred of them..Then we caught nothing for the next two weeks so we pulled out all the traps, that was a learning session for all of in the family, we set mouse traps later and took six of those in about a month so we were rodent free after that we would set traps of both kinds at three or four week intervals just to make sure we stayed rodent free in our chicken feed house.Mom felt much easier about leaving bread or other foods out on the table at night after that. It was strange we never saw any signs of them in our house and only on one occasion did we suspect they were around, Dad saw one of the large ones in the fireplace area of the kitchen and killed it with his 22 rifle one Saturday afternoon. That was our first clue that we had a problem, and the mess created in the feed house confirmed it.But my bro and I were determined to rid ourselves of these things and mom and dad had a few laughs at our dedication to eliminate them we were just kids but it was kinda our project to do it like we wanted to and mom and dad watched and let us do it.our way.and we got them all and continued to check that they didn't return.

My. Zip. Gun.

I By forty five I was very tired of getting my butt beat by the bully boys and the principal at school on the way to and from home, And at home! That was beginning to wear me down so I being a movie fan at the time(it was fairly safe in there) kinda liked the Bowery Boys way of doing things _ so I attempted to fabricate myself a zip gun a 22 caliber, using a 22 short bullet, I had seen one in one of the Bowery Boys movies in those days a box of 22 shorts fifty to a box was fifteen cents, so after many, many failures I finally got one to shoot, well and I showed that around town to the boys and demonstrated it a time or two and stuck in in my belt (unloaded of course) and within two days the bully boys started avoiding me completely (didn't faze my dad tho.). And for the first time I actually got my lips to heal up and quit bleeding for a new feeling. Things got quiet!! A new phase in my life at School.

My mom found my "zip" under my underwear in my dresser drawer and I explained it off as another way of killing frogs with the tiny miniature mustard seed type 22s shells that were there with it.(I had stopped using the 22 shorts and used the non lethal "snake" shot ones they were available at the same price.they looked larger than the "shorts" I have no idea what mom did with my "zipper" but it was gone.And I never saw it again, I did ask her where it was and all I got was,_ quote_"I didn't tell your

dad about that, so quit while you're ahead"____ YES MAM____
I said!

CARS 1950

Cars kinda slipped up on me, I had ridden in them all my
life, but never considered driving one until I was about fourteen
And really never tried to learn the complete process Until I was
fourteen in forty eight and 1/3 owner of a that model A flatbed
truck I knew how to repair them but that didn't qualify me to even
come close to driving, and the real hard facts were I Could not
drive one, So the time had come!!gotta learn how to drive__ the
one with a license at seventeen and the oldest of the three owners
of the truck so he gave us both driving lessons over in New Town
an area of the county that was sparsely populated, and I learned
it pretty quickly, and after the first month, we both gave up on
my buddy so I drove it a lot when out of the city limits where
there were no cops the licensed one drove it in town, downhill we
could get it up to fifty, loaded with stove wood going to Atlanta on
Saturday about forty five mph was top speed And after a few sales
in the AM we filled it up with gas at the twenty cents per gallon
gas station over in west Atlanta and after the day was over and we
headed for the swimming hole the other two would start hitting
the Mad Dog, So I took over the "wheel" and drove there. Later
on that spring I got my license and stretched my birthday a little,
I Was really fifteen And my license said eighteen, but now I was
somewhat more legal.than I Was before. And I got the job in the
ice cream room because I was eighteen, and Bought My First car
that thirty three Chrysler Windsor that spring and now I could
spread out my wings!!! And new territory's awaited me. __Lots I
Didn't Know Yet_But I Was on my way World!!Had to hide the
car, can't take it home that would be suicide, so I made a deal
with Mr, Ira Rainwater to park in his car shed, five houses up the
road from my house by the way Mr Rainwater's middle name

was Patrick So I.P. Rainwater was his real name I often wondered about his parents?. Don't You? What were They thinking?

PARTY ANIMALS 1948

After I became 14 years old I got invited to a classmates and another friends birthday party and summer outings at local parks and even some at the city swimming pool for swim parties some I attended and some I declined, it depended upon whether it was a boy or a girls party, At fourteen I was still being dressed like Klem kiddilehopper in overalls and flannel shirts and brogan shoes, the girls were more diplomatic than the boys which usually popped right up with the finger, that got his nose bleeding real quick, So _usually we were ask to leave before the party began by the mothers. Kinda hard to tell your mom that without making her feel bad. And after a few of these incident's its best to just don't go.

Or just pretend you went and talk about what a great time you had.to mom.It was hard to keep from crying sometimes when you are lying your butt off to your mom about the games we played there and how much fun you had. when you wish you really had the guts to tell her what really happened. How do you do that to your mom? it's not her fault, crying on the inside laughing on the outside_ Hard to do. Sometimes, guess I got some of that "pride" that my dad was always talking about, at times that's all I had to keep me going. my pride_and puberty__ made me do lots of things that maybe, Just maybe I should not have done or I should have done and didn't__It sure was a powerful motivator at that phase in my life.kids can be cruel to other kids. At. times, without realizing it.

And the very mention of sex at that period of time sure started the imagination and thoughts of what that was like to fogging up your brain, seems it was the main thing to anticipate for a long time and girls flirting with us did not eliminate it from our thoughts, some of the imagined scenarios were pretty graphic in our deranged little minds, it's a good thing they could not even think of what we were, or they would never have dated us without a bodyguard or gun, aw good old puberty, what a trip.

HOMESICK 1951

Hell, I knew we were poor!I didn't need it rubbed in my face at every turn by the "Haves" and that's why I took so many chances in my youth to improve my personal financial condition it was not that I was a bad kid, I was a proud and determined kid and, I didn't care who your Daddy was or what his position in life was or your goody goody attitude was about me. I did not care what you thought, save it, I had my own agenda and certain types of people, kids, and so _ called teachers were just thorns in my path and were there not to help or to make my life any easier, in fact they were blocking my progress I just had no idea where I was going or how to get there. So the day that I got booted from the hell in my School. to another place was a blessing in disguise I just didn't recognize it at first. But it was the start of another direction and I've been on it ever since!.as I grew older and looked back and remembered some of the events that occurred to me and the depravity that my family suffered, I came to realize that "it "was the fire that tempered me for the future in this ever changing world we live in today.some survive, some fail, it depends on how adaptable we are.never say never! Every. Tomorrow you get another chance! and I was ready to take it. That was my "Pride" talking again and this time it had really screwed up, but here it is boy! you sure did it this time! Now Deal with it, make something out of it if you can!!!!.Pride goes before the fall, I had heard.And I Just Fell and the next few months was Hell.! I was sad. And mad, Over in Alabama..and Homesick.!!! A long way from home!!!

BULL 1947

I got my chance to become a world famous bull rider At an early age about 13 as I recall thanks to my grandfather and a few of my first cousins, boys and girls together We were all over in grandpa's pasture walking along looking for wild grapes (muscadines) up in the big tall trees and had found a few but not enough for us all we could eat lots more than we could find, there were a few of his cattle wandering everywhere in the pasture and one young bull alone behind the rest so___ the discussion became about the bull and the riding of that particular bull most of the boys were all for ridding him but the problem was catching him, holding him, and getting on him, we have no rope and every time we tried to corner him he got past us and we had to catch up again, not an easy situation, the girls got way behind, but we stopped and waited on them, it was all a "show off" for the girls anyway, so we went deeper into the woods and momentarily lost sight of him then we were thru the woods into an area that at one time had been a roadway and a small creek flowed down into the far side of the woods and the remains of an old wooden bridge was still intact enough for me to climb up on it and I ask the boys to chase the bull up the creek and under the bridge and I would jump down onto the bull grab his ears and ride him__ yep,__ the boys ran him down into the creek and up under the bridge with no problem and as planned I dropped down onto the bull, that lasted almost 1/10th of one second and I was up with the birds and my landing had not been thoroughly thought out by me or seemingly anyone else because it was ugly! I heard the thump just before I felt it, the landing was not quite on my left hip or my backside it was kinda on both, and the pain was the first reminder of exactly how completely stupid that had been, the bull ran off about thirty yards and stood looking back at me and I swear it was laughing.

some one ran back to grandpa's and came back with ten of the uncles and a wheelbarrow to carry me back to the house, my bull riding days over before they began.I hurt for two weeks afterwards! Bareback bull riding is now officially off my things to do list.! Damn that hurt.

THE MOVIES 1946

Sometimes when I was eleven or so and my brother was eight or so there would not be even as much as a quarter that was in the house, and all the begging and pleading with mom to come up with even that amount was to no avail, it just was not there, in those days the "Capitola" brand of flour that mom used had tokens made of aluminum in a sack of flour, the ten lb sack only had one token, but the twenty five lb sack had two tokens, mom always got the big ones, so after a search of the kitchen, usually we could come up with a few tokens, so at our age and below 2 tokens got you into the movies, I never learned what the redemption value was to the movie theater was but it was to us kids then a real bonus, only two token per person, in a sack of flour!!

_Even well armed with the appropriate fees to get in we still went around back of the building to see if either of the fire escape doors were ajar or open for ventilation because A/Cond. Was unheard of then, if so we would sneak in and save the tokens for another day And without those tokens we would never been allowed to go, if it was Saturday then the late show begin at midnight, that was normally the scary ones that we really wanted to see, so we had to either hide,,, or go to the fire doors while the original movie was on and place a small rock in the door so it would not close tightly, and wait until the movie started and sneak back in, lot of the time there was fifty five people or more watching the late movie and only maybe twenty paid tickets. The owners went home for the night at midnight, and the camera operator was up overhead in the camera room and the back doors were propped wide open to let it cool off in there and anyone could just wait until they saw the owners leave and just walk in, l So if we had tokens, we had to hide them where they would not be found and the cemetery was one place mom and dad would not be looking.__ But the movies was the only type of recreation that we got, some of us had a very drab lives we were forced to live with day after day, a lot of kids ran away from home, some were found and some were not, a girl that I knew ran away when she was fifteen and wrote to her mom from California three years later. Boys were usually not so lucky as girls when they ran away from poverty and hard work, I always said that girls ran away "To "something_ and boys ran away "From" something. And that was the biggest reason boys were caught.and the girls were not. Poverty and boredom A bad combination! Makes Good people do Bad things, It has not gone away Today its just been renamed

My dad did not live long enough to see any of his seven children attain any degree of success in his life, three packs of Camel cigarettes and a pint of whiskey a day and far too much brake dust inhaled into his lungs six days a week for years ruined his health and his early death put my mom on a new and different course on life, the ones still at home when he died grew up and mom got to see her hard work and prayers for her kids come to far more than she had hoped and prayed for, and most of us are just about as happy as we want to be in our own lives.today __Times have changed...

YARD BALL1949

Recess" that was always the time we were all waiting on, in class. we didn't have a fancy gym. Or much room for a lot of students only a few of the best ever got to play anything, So you can imagine what some of thought and felt every one was not good at sports, There was a baseball field on the south side of the school and a basketball court on the east side all dirt and some 8_10 stone steps to sit on to observe both, those were also where the poor "left out" boys and most of the girls sat, and wished, and cheered, or chatted __ Seems like you only got fifteen mins. In morning and evening recess, so a full game of either was not possible soccer had not been invented yet or we would have needed more room usually a ball game took at least three hours to get in nine innings and basket ball game could end in a 0_0 tie in fifteen mins.So it was kick the foot ball with ten on each end of the basketball court back and forth.

There was one girl Bobbe. that could kick the cover off a football we all moved back if it was coming our way if she was kicking it, many boys were envious of the way and the distance she could kick a football, and so was I.. Too bad we didn't have a football team she would have "Lettered not only" in that for sure but she could hit a baseball out of sight If she wanted to play ball with us boys, she got "Chosen" quickly! She was one of the more athletic girls in our school, and her brother was an excellent baseball player, and played on the city team. Most all the little towns and even communities had a ball team and my town had a nice baseball field (and I think mister Nap Rucker had a lot to do with that somehow) there were a few serious games played on Sunday afternoon at times. That were worth the 50 cents it cost to get in.the gate.

Billy 1946

I was up in my hometown one Saturday evening before dark I was hanging out with a friend of mine that had the only cab company in town, he started it in his own car, he was about twenty four years old and just out of the army and every one knew Bill, he was a good guy, and everyone liked him, we were just sitting in his car b/sing when he said, Boy I could use a nice "T"Bone__ and I had no idea what he meant by that so I ask what a T Bone was, you mean you never had a steak? He ask and no I never had___ so he said "Hang on a minute," and called his wife, told her he was going to eat, be back in a while, and we went to a Restaurant and he bought me my first steak, that was a treat I had never experienced, and cost Bill two bucks and i returned that favor a few years later, his cab company flourished in the coming years and that was good because Bill was a nice person.___But in the summers that followed when I was in Atlanta I did partake some good and some not so good steaks, that was about the same time I learned about lobster also, a new and exciting group of seafood that was never served at home, my horizons were expanding. expanding you.

Bottled beer was another new thing, around town but "still beer". Was available by the quart at times(this was the corn mash beer that was boiled to make moonshine) it was a little stronger than store bought beer, and that made bottled beer taste weird. Another treat was pork barbecue, (also known by the letter "Q") there was some available in town down in the black section of town on Saturday nights only, but we were not too welcome to go there and sit and eat, for the white folks it had to be "To Go" it was an open air type eating area with picnic style tables with limited seating anyway, so we took no offence to the reverse discriminations that prevailed at the time, they also had some "home brew" that was a type of beer that would make you stand up & slap your grandma, and it was real good with the Q we usually got ours early in the evening, before the trouble started down there, and the cops closed it down before ten some Saturday nights.before the free for alls broke out and the cutting and shooting began. They seemed to have lots of trouble down there! Darn good Q tho. Who ever the cook was knew his Q And the price was right. And we kids appreciated that..They had pork and chicken most of the time if you got there early.

AUTO WRECKS 1950

I never figured out why so many of the young boys in town were involved in auto accidents, and so many of them died, it seemed that almost every Saturday night someone else that I knew was killed in a wreck, I often wondered if they were drinking or just showing off normally if the race track was open my friends and I were on the race track speeding he and I were racing up on the dirt track, not out on the road, I would on occasion later in age, make the new road race from Canton Ga. To North Atlanta race about midnight Saturday night, that was about as stupid as I got on the highways, and that was exciting for a few times, but it was basically just a donation, To this bunch of guys, I never had anything that would even begin to run with this bunch.of nuts. And they were all older and more of them had some really fast cars than us wannabes it took big money to run with them.___ But it was exciting occasionally, but not a regular habit.Most of them were either chicken farmers, or bootleggers, Those cars they had cost big bucks.Not my league, for sure.

BOOK REPORTS 1946

My 5th grade teacher gave the class a summer reading program to read at least ten books and to write a book report of at least two pages on each book read. Now, book reports were not one of my favorites, however reading was and still is one of the most enjoyable pastimes' that I can think of, I read with a passion, anything and many topics are still of interest to me. At the first day on the new term of school she came into the 6th grade room and ask the students to turn in our book reports very few of the twenty five or so had completed the reports, some had different excuses for not having them done, I however turned in forty book reports, and needless to say she looked surprised and ask me if that was supposed to be funny, and I tried to assure her that I had indeed read that many books over the summer and, had written those reports in earnest, she accepted them and walked away back to her classroom, That afternoon when I got home, my mom said that my teacher had called her that afternoon and ask if she knew anything of this, and mom told her that I was indeed a reader and had carried some sort of book with me most of the time all summer, and would not be surprised if I had read all those, and that I did write something about each of them, and that she had read some of them that I had left laying about the house.so yes she thought. Perhaps I did.

I was surprised when she gave me a certificate of award for "Reading" that summer, I still have it today. I was so proud of that it was a "first" for me. No teacher had ever given me any recognition for anything except being a pest and impudent. Was it me? Or was it them? I still don't know! I always mostly got treated by most teachers at the time like a smart ass or an idiot. And was a C or D student.

And after the "ordeal". At my hometown school and the resulting year or so I was usually exempt from quarterly exams after the first quarter, and was an almost all "A" Student at my new school, and. I Was treated like a human being, with courtesy and respect, not a hooligan and an Idiot. Does the clothes that we wear make that much difference? I did have more and newer trendier clothes at the time and enjoyed attending school then, more than at any time in my life. It was a new world,

That was basically the only difference, between the two schools and myself, I did dress better and was more relaxed and of course the teaching staff was worlds apart, and so was the techniques used to teach us.that was more apparent than anything else to me, they actually cared about us as a person.and made learning a pleasure.and in that state of mind made it also easier to learn, I was more relaxed and felt that these people were here to help me, not setting me up for punishment of some sort or just waiting for me to screw up some way, actually I was on guard at my old school all the time from the teaching staff, I did not trust any of them. And I'm sure the feeling was mutual! They had worked hard to make it that way. So much for what I learned at that School. As the school got better in the future I'm sure so did the students, but it was primitive while I was there and I would never send my children there, I would have moved.

STICKING. IT OUT

I have often wondered what happened to the people who "Stuck it out" at the old high school if their education there helped or prevented them from attaining their true potential in life Sadly most of the boys of my age that I grew up with have all died and the half dozen girls that I have located that are still with us were all married soon after finishing school, They and their families have seen the results in their own children that accomplished so much more so much sooner than they did and that is attributed that to fact that the times have changed for the better and that was left all of that up to their husband and, wherever they got their education at the time and the subject of "Could you have had a more fulfilling life" having a better quality of education has not been a subject that they ever cared about.or are willing to discuss this with me at this point in their life,_its too late. Was the answer I got, and they are correct, and each of them feel content with the life they have led. It was a free choice on their part. "But What If."

You never know how much you need a good education until you need it, and don't have it, and a very good part of your life just did not never, ever happen. That could have changed your whole life for the better. Its not the money, its what you could enjoy and be happiest at doing, while making money. Unfortunately a lot of people never find that combination in their lives "without that all important education" And if your school that you attended in your childhood did not spark your interest, you were cheated out of

Your opportunity to be successful in life. Teaching is the art to pique your interest in Everything, or Anything, to challenge you to greater things in life. My first ten years in school were employed to conquer me, Not to teach me!, I got a three year Education at my new high School, I learned more information that I have used,

Out of school Than I ever did in school, I don't blame the school, it was the staff, The Teachers.and the school board, maybe they could not afford good professional staff, I don't know why, I only know what my personal results were____Tragic almost ruined my complete life. Trying. To survive.!

puberty's changes in attitude would now create more contemptuous behavior than before, it's the male compulsive urge to get even._ and another problem is created right or wrong there it is!!!and things deteriorate from then on to the explosion.-- And the adults wonder why!. Puberty alone is hard to contend with as a youth.-_-, add to that the deprivation of poverty, --and the delirium of pride in ourselves_ and someone has a serious problem on their hands!!!! Not necessarily the solution that was expected by the teachers and staff, puberty is not an equal opportunity adjustment to be able to see the end result of becoming a man or woman _ its a few years of near insanity and changes from a child to an adult,__piece of cake for some,__pure hell for others!!!.and sadly I fell into that group!

I guess that my mom had so many of us that she had a full time job just dealing with the younger children that she had little time to pay too much attention to the older ones that were capable of mostly caring for ourselves, so we were basically on our own most of the time, one of the free range style kids of my day.and my excuse for always being able to satisfied her that I was OK was that I was playing baseball at the ballpark with others of my age, I was gone from home most of the time, and put in my appearance just before dad got home at night, that kept the controversy down as to my deeds for the day, as long as my chores were done and homework for school was finished I was fairly safe from the lessons to be learned the hard way from switch, or dads belt.

Baseball covered my behind rather well because mom never came looking for me there, while I was elsewhere getting our stove wood cut over at the sawdust pile or even making our purchases of moonshine to mix with the stove wood for the busy, Saturdays we were peddling our wares in Atlanta on Saturday, those were the ball games that we played out of town she was told, and I guess she thought that was a fact, because I played baseball almost every day in the afternoons and all day on Saturday, somewhere, I definitely led a charmed life in that area with mom, I don't think she would have approved of me being involved in my real efforts at my age and most likely none of the company that I had been associated with, and definitely not off down in Atlanta selling booze in the areas that we worked in every Saturday morning.that kind of news was not for moms ears, if the truth had been known, between the two of them, I would most likely still be confined to a wheelchair.

I wish that I had not wasted so much energy back then, perhaps I would have more today. At least I was not concerned with mischief like some of the boys around town, I was more interested in the money aspect of creating a better life for my own reasons, I had not been able to have any pride in my social standing ever!!and I wanted to elevate that, by the time I was twelve I knew that if I was to be able to be one of the "In" group at school, that it was! up to me to do it, overalls and brogan shoes and checkered shirts did not get it. I was too proud to steal, so I worked for it, and although my methods were crude it was the fast way to get what I wanted with the least amount of dishonesty. But it still had to be above suspicion from my parents, because it would not be allowed, and I knew it.so which is worse, a thief Or a liar? I covered my tracks pretty well so as not to get caught in lies that were to complicated, so I kept it simple, I'm playing baseball, a lot!!!and you hate yourself for doing this, but you really have to after you are committed, and the other two guys that are in this project with you are counting on your help every day, and if its to be a three way split on the proceeds I'm committed to my part of the work. living completely different lives at that age was so difficult at times, it was just almost not real. And I was hard headed to begin with, and this message I'm getting from my teachers that I should act my age, when what I'm doing, and the people that I'm dealing with as a semi adult already in the real world, every weekend was a difficult task and we boys worked hard most week afternoons preparing for Saturdays and they were hard, long and extremely tiring, I was offended, but I had to hide that emotion or it would escalate into something else! Little did they know.

I guess I really was too big for my britches., no respect!, just another dumb ass kid.with big ideas day dreaming my life away, if they only knew, sometimes it was difficult to keep quiet! I was at least trying to cure the poverty portion of my busy life. I'm glad that my mom and dad never knew some of the things that I did back in those days it would have shocked and hurt. them terribly.However we did a lot of charitable things for some of the less fortunate older people in our community that no one except the recipients ever knew about. We helped when we could, and without being asked.we knew what need was,.and we knew what pride was.and we knew some of those those old. People would never ask. For help.----but they did thank us for our kindness.that, was our reward when we were just kids.

TAKING A WIFE

My ice cream.route eventually became. A. dating game in time, also, because I had met a. Shy sweet young. Girl Margaret with lots of brothers and they all loved ice cream, but had no money, but silly me I gave them some anyway, her oldest brother wanted a job helping me in in the late afternoon rush hours before dark, so we worked together for a few weeks, and as the sales dropped off as evenings got cooler, I spent more time with, his sister, and we dated all fall and winter and and were married the thirtieth of April the next year, we had three children, two boys one girl we were married for twenty five years and six months, before ending it.in Arizona thru mutual agreement, we had taken different paths, later in our lives, all our children had grown up, married and left home.Our song had been sung, time for recess.

DEDICATIONS TO

THE. GIRLS IN MY LIFE
HELEN----my first love.
RUTH------her cousin
EDNA-----her sweet little sister
CHAROLETTE----my second love
MARGARET----- my first wife for 25 years
ROSEMARY----my second wife for 38 years
NEVA----daughter # 1
VERONICA-----daughter# 2
MARY LOU.----my mom
LEONA----my wonderful mother inlaw.
KAREN ---- my only sister in law
AND AND TO MY FIVE CHILDREN, DAVID,
NEVA, DANNY, VERONICA, AND JOE.

Printed in the United States
By Bookmasters